PK

Also by Cameron Lee:
Life in a Glass House (with Jack Balswick)

Helping Pastors' Kids Through Their Identity Crisis

PK

CAMERON LEE

ZondervanPublishingHouse

Academic and Professional Books

Grand Rapids, Michigan

A Division of HarperCollins*Publishers*

PK: Helping Pastors' Kids Through Their Identity Crisis
Copyright © 1992 by Cameron Lee

Requests for information should be addressed to:
Zondervan Publishing House
Academic and Professional Books
Grand Rapids, Michigan 49530

Library of Congress Cataloging-in-Publication Data

Lee, Cameron.
    PK : helping pastors' kids through their identity crisis / Cameron Lee.
      p.   cm.
    Includes bibliographical references and index.
    ISBN 0-310-58451-5
    1. Children of clergy—Psychology. 2. Identity (Psychology) I. Title.
    BV4396.L45   1992   92-12684
    253'.2—dc20   CIP

Edited by James E. Ruark
Cover design by Jack Foster

Printed in the United States of America

92 93 94 95 96 97 / CH / 10 9 8 7 6 5 4 3 2 1

Contents

Foreword

Editors are among the people who work behind the scenes to help an author's book get into print in a pleasing and readable form. Each book is different, and some books come to have special meaning to editors for professional reasons. But the reason that *PK* stands out for me is personal. I am a pastor's kid, and I have waited a long time for such a book as this.

I am not one of the hundred PKs whom Cameron Lee studied in his research, yet I see myself on every page. Years ago I came to terms with my past—*what* I am. But in reading this book I have learned a great deal about the *why*. Cameron Lee demystifies the perplexing questions of personhood in the parsonage. In the concepts of "boundaries" and "social ecology" he gives handles to what happens in the clergy family and the church that makes a PK's life unique and, too often, frangible. His use of the metaphor of the theater, viewing PKs as involuntary actors at center stage in the unfolding drama of church life, is instructive and enlightening.

Admittedly, others grow up in "glass houses"—the children of celebrities, politicians, and psychiatrists, for example. We meet some of them in these pages and learn from their insights also. But the religious context for pastors' kids tends to make their problems more severe because of the overtones of morality and spirituality attached to them.

It is inevitable, perhaps, that a great deal more is said in this book about the pain than the privileges of being a PK. The struggles bring a sense of urgency and are more difficult to understand. Jesus said, "It is not the healthy who need a doctor, but the sick."

In retrospect, it seems that the privileges I enjoyed while growing up far outweighed the pain I endured. Surely my pain did not seem as great as that of many of the pastors' kids who speak—sometimes in bitter tones—in this book. Was my experience exceptional, especially in the fundamentalist world in which I grew up? I fear as much. I believe my parents did more than many clergy families I knew to preserve a degree of privacy and maintain the suitable boundaries that Cameron Lee writes about.

It is important to see the flaws in the social ecology of pastors' kids as a contemporary problem and not merely dusty history. Despite a growing awareness of relational needs and "warm fuzzies" in many churches over the last thirty years or so, struggles persist for many PKs today. The PKs who speak out in these pages include a number in their teens who are still living with their clergy parents. So we must conclude that the potential for pain has not been alleviated enough. There is as much need for *PK* now as ever.

To pastors' kids who are still hurting, *PK* brings a message of healing through compassionate understanding. To clergy parents, Dr. Lee points the way toward wholesome respect that will enrich family life in the manse. To parishioners and other readers, this book offers a much-needed corrective to church life that will help the body of Christ become more like what it was meant to be.

PK is okay. PKs are okay.

—*James E. Ruark*

Preface

It is Sunday morning. You are visiting a certain church for the first time, waiting out in front of the sanctuary for the friend who invited you. A minute later, you catch sight of your friend, and together you pass through the narthex to enter the sanctuary. Your friend nods toward a teenager talking and laughing nearby with other teenagers. "See her?" your friend asks. "That's our pastor's daughter."

Immediately the mind goes into gear. What do you expect the pastor's daughter to look like? How do you expect her to behave? What kind of a person do you think she is? Would it make any difference if it were the pastor's son instead of the daughter?

The children of ministers, commonly known as "pastors' kids," "preachers' kids," or "PKs" for short, will tell you that the public in general, and church members in particular, often have common expectations of their behavior and character. Sometimes there is only minor pressure to conform, and the minister's child may view parishioners' expectations with a certain amount of amusement. In other cases, expectations can be so conspicuous that PKs may feel that how others relate to them is based more on images, stereotypes, distortions, or denials than on reality. In such situations, some PKs feel compelled to break from the stereotypes and behave in seemingly "uncharacteristic" ways. Others may learn to "play the part" and become adept at putting on whatever face they are expected to wear in public gatherings.

Whence come these expectations? How important are they in the lives of PKs? These are complex questions, and the published literature is of little help. In 1989, my colleague Jack Balswick and I wrote *Life in a Glass House*, an examination of the social and emotional world of clergy families based on a survey study. Only one chapter of that book was devoted exclusively to ministers' children. As we combed through the literature, we were struck by the virtual absence of research on the children of clergy. There were a few scattered

references, most of them snippets from the lives of PKs, written by
their parents for the benefit of other clergy. Little systematic research,
however, has been done. This lack is striking when one considers the
prevalence of PK stereotypes and their effect on ministers' families.

This book is an initial attempt to fulfill the need for formal
research. Here PKs "tell it like it is," through first-person accounts
culled from surveys, interviews, and correspondence with more than a
hundred children of ministers. These people have consented to let us
peer into their private lives in the hope that others may understand
what it means to be a pastor's child. They represent childhoods spent
in more than thirty states in the United States, Australia, and several
other countries. They range in age from their early teens to their mid-
fifties. Their parents have ministered in more than twenty denominations, in everything from tiny rural congregations to urban super-
churches. Some of the PKs have gone into parish ministry themselves.
Where possible, this information is supplemented by stories gleaned
from other sources, including articles and biographies.

As in *Life in a Glass House*, the ministers cited in this book are
assumed to be men. This is only because the PKs who participated in
this study came from families in which this was true, with only one or
two exceptions, and in those, both the father and mother were
ordained ministers. Perhaps future research will allow us to ask what
difference it would make to PKs to have Mom as the sole ordained
minister in the home!

There are many similarities in their stories, yet many differences
as well. One major purpose of this book is to convey a simple point: If
you really want to understand how PKs live, simplistic stereotypes
have little value. Accordingly, I will continue the "ecological"
perspective begun in *Life in a Glass House*. Simply put, a social-
ecological stance means that individuals and their behavior must be
understood in terms of how they interact with their social environments and cannot be fully understood apart from such real-life
contexts. This means that ministers' children cannot be understood
simply in individual terms. Rather, they are born into families, and
these families minister closely to churches. Whom the PKs become
depends not only on their inborn traits and qualities, but also on the
characteristics of their families and the congregations they serve. Take
a PK with a happy childhood and move him to a different congregation, and the whole picture may change for the worse. Take another,
unhappy with her situation, and change the interaction with her
parents, and the scene may brighten up. Still another, who seems well-

adjusted in his earlier years, may cause quite a storm when he becomes a teenager.

I have taken great pains to safeguard the identities of the PKs whose stories appear within these pages. Some of the PKs I interviewed were reluctant to participate because they did not know me, and experience has taught them to be cautious of giving their trust. To protect that trust, I have altered or left out names, places, dates, and references to family characteristics. In some cases stories have been combined, while in others they have been divided. In every case, however, I have endeavored to remain as true as possible to the stories the PKs have chosen to tell.

Are you planning to enter the ministry, or are you already in the ministry but do not yet have children? I hope this book will help you anticipate what your children may face. Are you already raising children during your ministry? I hope the stories here will help your relationship with them. It is important to remember that, public and personal expectations to the contrary, good parenting skills are not automatically conferred upon ordination! As a minister you bring the same kinds of emotional freight to parenting as anyone else. If there have been conflicts between you and your children, let the PKs who speak here build a thoughtful bridge between you.

Are you an involved member of a local congregation? Ask yourself what you can do to make the lives of clergy families less stressful and the experiences of PKs more rewarding. Do you teach or work with clergy or their families professionally? You may well have many PKs either in your classrooms or counseling offices. Here is a glimpse into their childhood struggles and victories.

This book is written most of all, however, for the PKs themselves. Are you the child of a minister? If your experience has been positive, I hope this book will allow you to celebrate your childhood and understand those whose experiences have been less fortunate. If your upbringing in the glass house has been a negative experience, my prayer is that this book will bring some healing—at the very least, reveal that you are not alone.

To all the ministers' children who took the time and risks to share their lives with me, thank you. This book is dedicated to you.

Acknowledgments

No book can be written in a vacuum, especially one like this. I am immensely indebted to the many clergy children whose stories and comments fill these pages. I hope that what I have written here will be worthy of their trust.

I also wish to thank many others who have helped in different ways to bring this project to fruition: to Mike Smith, whose editorial vision brought the book to the drawing board in the first place; to Rob and Liz Bailey and their sons, Nathan and Bretlyn, for their invaluable assistance in collecting data in Australia; to Marty Seitz, who helped with the data collection in the United States; to Fuller Theological Seminary, for the sabbatical leave needed to conduct the research; to my wife and children, who patiently and lovingly endured while Daddy had to write another book; to our neighbors, Doug and Kathy Leo, who graciously left for an extended vacation while I commandeered their dining table to finish the manuscript; and finally, to Jim Ruark, for his usual enthusiasm and finesse in his role as editor.

The Drama

CHAPTER ONE

Who Am I, Really?

Who is the "pastor's kid," the so-called PK?

That is the question many PKs have asked themselves: Who am I? The daughters and sons of clergy live in a complex social world. Their childhood is lived within the larger, extended family of a local congregation. It is a life in the public eye, with the accompanying mixture of religious and personal expectations. If it is difficult for many contemporary youth to "find themselves," the search can be even more complicated for pastors' children. On the one hand, a consistently lived-out ministry in the midst of a supportive congregation provides a steady vision and stable social context. On the other hand, congregations frequently behave in capricious and self-contradictory ways, much as dysfunctional families do. In these cases, a PK's quest for self-identity may be difficult indeed.

Many PKs recount their early years with great affection for their families, and some extend this affection to the congregations their parents served. They consider their childhoods normal, even "boring." Still, many who have these positive experiences consider themselves a minority, judging from other PKs they have known or the stereotypes that they themselves hold. Some PKs are bitter or resentful, often deeply ambivalent about the church. I assured one minister's daughter, for example, that many other pastors' children truly enjoyed childhood. Her unflinching response: "They're denying something." In more extreme cases, some have left the church entirely or have embraced some other form of spirituality such as one of the New Age groups.

The purpose of this book is not to proclaim that it is either "good" or "bad" to be raised in a clergy family. Admittedly, I am more concerned for those who have had painful experiences, and thus I have put greater emphasis on understanding and healing the negatives than on celebrating the positives. Generalizations of "good" and "bad," however, ignore the multitude of factors that shape any childhood, PK's or not. Therefore I want us to look at ministers' children through the lens of a social ecology in order to appreciate how the quality of their lives is shaped by their interaction with the social environment. For clergy families in particular, more than with most professions, the boundaries between the "outside" social environment and the family's private life are altogether too ambiguous.

Despite the differences in ministers' homes, some stereotypes persist and are carelessly applied. Certainly PKs themselves frequently have a sense of their "specialness," of being different from other children. Some resent being different, as one minister's daughter told me: "I despised the fact that we were not ordinary people, and I think that is the PK 'thing.' "

Asking where these stereotypes originated is a chicken-or-egg question. But it is surely the social context that maintains them. One does not usually find such consistent expectations of the children of lawyers or teachers or accountants or plumbers or any other profession or occupation. In other families, the parents' vocations are usually regarded as playing only a minor role in their children's lives. But as the very existence of the term "PK" indicates, there is a stereotyped expectation that the children of ministers are somehow different.

OCCUPATIONAL HAZARDS

Why does it matter that one's parents are ministers? Thomas Maeder, who has written about the children of psychiatrists, gives us a clue. He observes that the rule that seems to separate professional life from the home does not hold for all families. The most notable exceptions, he writes, are clergy and psychotherapists:

> Religion and psychotherapy are not merely occupations, . . . nor are they professions easily left at the office when one goes home. Both are philosophical systems deeply concerned with the daily lives and social interactions of people; and in both cases their practitioners are expected, to a greater or lesser extent, to embody the principles they espouse. Their jobs become inseparable from their identities, and therefore become part of their families' identities as well.[1]

The minister, to many, is supposed to be a paragon of moral virtue. Church members look to their ministers for guidance and direction in all spheres of life. Indeed, as clergy and PKs alike will tell you, some of the flock seem nearly incapable of making the most routine decisions regarding church matters (and sometimes personal matters) without the pastor's blessing. But what if all is not well in the clergy home? What church members see (or think they see!) of the minister's family life can easily tarnish the idealized image of their spiritual leader. What they see includes the behavior of the minister's children.

Maeder's comment about identity is particularly important. It is one thing for the pastor or even the pastor's spouse to be confronted with the expectations of ministry life. They are adults: They have chosen their profession, and to a greater or lesser extent it is already consistent with some aspect of their identity. This is not the case with their children. The offspring have no choice in the matter, for they are born into an environment of their parents' choosing. Their search for identity takes place in a context in which people already have stereotyped expectations of who they will or must be, often before they have truly had the chance to find out who they are. One adult PK who has struggled with whether or not to remain in the ministry himself sums up the conflict: "There is a tension between who I know I am, who I want to be as a person, and who the local church expects me to be."

There are, I believe, important differences between psychiatrists' children and PKs. First, many PKs find it difficult to answer the question "Where are you from?" because they have moved frequently in childhood. One evangelist's son reported that during his preschool years alone, he and his family lived in well over one hundred cities. Another PK had more than a dozen addresses in ten years, spending no more than four years in one place. This kind of mobility at crucial times in a child's life can make it difficult to establish and maintain normal friendships, and it increases the PK's dependence on the family.

The second difference is more crucial. Ministers' children are more visible than those of psychiatrists. Although there are exceptions, as Maeder himself documents, the professional boundaries of psychotherapeutic practice can help shield the psychiatrist's child from the intrusions of curious patients. Not so the clergy, particularly those who live in parsonages on church grounds. Their lives are more akin to those of media celebrities who become public property for thousands of adoring fans. The congregation, of course, may not number into the thousands, but the intrusive sense of being put on a pedestal, of being "owned" by the group, is much the same.

Celebrity parents have chosen their fame, while their children are born into it. Adults may find ways to cope with the intrusions of fans, but the children need help with this problem. Kathy Cronkite has written passionately about her life as the daughter of the television journalist Walter Cronkite:

> "What is it like to be Walter Cronkite's daughter?" Of all the questions I've had to deal with since childhood, I've found that question the most common and annoying. . . . I've heard all the related questions and can answer them, in order, before they're asked. They fall into two categories: curiosity about how foreign and special my life must be . . . and an attempt to get to know the idol better through me. . . . I find both types of questions to be personally disparaging. The former makes me feel like a caterpillar in a jar, and the latter attempts to make me a spokesperson for my father, without concern for my own thoughts or identity.[2]

Here is a child beset by the curiosity of an adoring public. What she quickly learns, however, is that behind the questions there is no real desire to hear her response, but only the wishes of fans to draw closer to the object of their adulation.

Ministers' children describe similar experiences. One pastor's son told of the numerous times that starry-eyed parishioners had asked him, "What's it like to live with your dad?" Privately the son thinks his father is "so heavenly minded he is no earthly good." But before he can formulate an appropriate response, the parishioner fills in the blank: "It must be wonderful." The son is left with the feeling that the well-meaning church member never really wanted to know the answer anyway. He feels frustrated at being denied an opportunity to say what he feels, and the encounter becomes one more instance of feeling that nobody really wants to know him. The focus is on the star of the show, the idol, and the son is left to feel like an appendage. This points up again the crucial issue for both PKs and the children of celebrities: the search for self-identity. Kathy Cronkite writes:

> It is the insensitivity of well-meaning fans that is most destructive to the children of the famous and that helps create and perpetuate the lack of discrete identity that we must live with.[3]

Adoration, however, is only one side of the story. Published stories of celebrities teach us that disappointed or disillusioned fans can be downright vicious. PKs may experience that same kind of malice:

> ■ Everything you do is open to the public. If someone were to ask me what it's like to be a minister's kid, I'd say it's like being a celebrity. You're open to the public, you have expectations, and when you don't fulfill them, you're scrutinized, you're slammed, you get thrown into the *Enquirer* or thrown into church gossip.

Other PKs resent the morbid curiosity of the congregation: "People want the dirt. If you could write a tabloid for our church, it would sell like hotcakes."

THE PROBLEM OF IDENTITY

The issue of identity is central for PKs. Their parents are local celebrities, if not national. Moreover, their fame is coupled with moral expectations consistent with the profession. Young children may be repeatedly impressed to believe that their parents are special and larger than life. Most children begin with these feelings, but eventually their perceptions of their parents become more realistic and less idealistic. But what if others continue to view their parents with halos? And what if the parents themselves want to be viewed this way? If realistic perceptions of Mom and Dad are not encouraged, the children will have a difficult time building realistic identities themselves.

So far I have used the term *identity* somewhat loosely. Indeed, the term is difficult to define. It has to do with an internal sense of sameness, a feeling of continuity between past and present. It is an answer to the question, "Who am I?"—not in my private self only, but in relationship to others who either support or challenge this self-concept.

A few decades ago, the term *identity crisis* became the watchword of an entire generation of youth, and it has been a staple of adolescent psychology ever since. Erik Erikson, the psychoanalyst who popularized the phrase, viewed the formation of identity as the pivotal task of human development.[4] In essence Erikson saw the often stormy teenage years as a critical stage during which people make a necessary transition from childhood into adult life. Adolescents are struggling to make sense of the variety of their childhood experiences, to pull them together into a meaningful whole under the umbrella of a coherent sense of self-identity. Erikson writes:

> The wholeness to be achieved at this stage I have called a sense of inner identity. The young person, in order to experience wholeness, must feel a progressive continuity between that which he has come to be during the long years of childhood and that which he promises to become in the anticipated future; between that which he conceives himself to be and that which he perceives others to see in him and expect of him.[5]

As human beings we share a drive for "ego-synthesis," as Erikson has called it. It is a fundamental motive force, our continuing quest for a self-concept that orders our experience and gives meaning and coherence to our life histories. The teenager draws together the threads of a tentative identity that is to be tested in the crucible of adulthood as he or she moves into intimate commitments and career and family decisions.

It is crucial that we do not overlook Erikson's social and cultural emphasis. An individual's identity is not formed in a vacuum. Children acquire the basic building blocks through successful interactions with an ever-widening circle of other people. Our earliest lessons are learned through parents and siblings; later we must integrate experiences with other relatives, teachers, and peers. Through these experiences come such crucial elements of identity as a willingness to engage in relationships; an ability to anticipate and experiment with different roles; the ability to identify what can or needs to be done, and the confidence to do it; and so on. These are, in broad strokes, the "stuff" of identity in Erikson's model. The "shape" of identity may be drawn from bits and pieces of social models derived from these numerous sources and from the culture at large.

To be functional, the sense of identity must integrate the events and relationships of a person's life in a way that fits with the values of his or her social group. Teenagers should be expected to struggle with these issues. Usually there is a period of time in which the social group recognizes that the adolescent needs some room to experiment, to think new thoughts, to try on new values and new identifications. Erikson calls this period the "psychosocial moratorium," and he considers it necessary to identity formation.

This stage is a critical time when PKs' evaluations of their childhood become set in one direction or another. Those who evaluate their past in a fairly positive light appear to have been given some free rein in the development of their sense of self. For the rest, the degree of negativity seems directly proportional to the degree of rigidity and restrictiveness given to their roles as PKs. The extension of the parents' professional identity to the children can happen in such a way that the PKs feel no alternatives are offered, that people cannot or will not see them as individuals. Again, this also holds true for celebrity children:

> It is difficult having two lives, two identities. I can't be just Kathy, who goes on dates and gets married and flunks history, because I'm Kathy, Walter Cronkite's daughter, who goes on dates and gets married (with attendant press) and—what? Flunks history? Granted, it makes an amusing anecdote, it may even make a not-so-amusing psychological point about rebellion, but

couldn't it also be just that I'm not very good at history? Where does Walter's daughter stop and Kathy begin?[6]

Would anyone care if someone else in the class flunked history? Why is it even "amusing"? The frustration for children in Kathy's situation lies in being constantly confronted by people who already think they know who you are because they know who your parents are. It is the experience of being boxed, labeled, stamped, and categorized. It is the feeling of being depersonalized, because you are not seen as a person in your own right, but merely an extension of your parents. Alyene Porter writes:

> No preacher's child can ever have a feeling of anonymity. Even now, as a woman, when I walk into a strange church two thousand miles from home, I can feel eyes directed toward me and hear a whispered echo, "That's the preacher's daughter." And from that moment every move must befit such a niche in life.[7]

There is something keenly intrusive about having your identity "packaged" in this way. Many PKs tolerate the role in their earlier years, sometimes even playing it to their advantage. As they near adolescence, however, these same children begin to feel a bind in their ability to create a sense of individuality.

> ■ And so it was for years: I was "Pastor Hamilton's son, Brian," not just "Brian." It was at this time of trying to discover if my real name contained four words or not, that I realized that I was becoming increasingly ambivalent about being the son of a "man of God." I began to struggle in earnest with what every child of a minister must struggle with—developing a sense of self.

For some PKs, the development of self-identity is not completed until later, when they have left the church environment. One minister's daughter found the anonymity afforded by college a welcome change from living in her father's shadow:

> ■ When I came to college, I realized I didn't like to tell people my last name. It meant that I was instantly identified as being my father's daughter. Not having a name means I won't be stereotyped and you won't think you know who I am. I'm getting over that because no one here knows my father or cares. It's wonderful! I guess I struggled for an individual identity—I didn't show it to many church people anyway. I had a teacher who always called me by my first *and* last name. Everyone else in the class was Mary or Jane or John or Steve, but I was Pastor Ray's daughter, so I had a first and last name. Might as well have tattooed it on my body.

Nor is standing in the shadow of publicly revered parents the only barrier to identifying self. Younger children often look up to older

siblings much as they look up to their parents. When an older brother
or sister has assumed the "proper" PK role and played it well, it puts
one more obstacle in the way. Everywhere one goes—in the family, in
church, even in college—it seems that the talented older sibling has
already been there, and the younger has yet another standard to live up
to, regardless of personal traits and abilities.

"Alan," a minister's son, was blessed with talents that were
valued by his parents and the congregations in which he was raised.
His younger sister, however, was not equally gifted. It was hard for her
to find a sphere in which to excel and earn praise, since her older
siblings seemed to be more talented and had already taken the available
options. What made it worse was to be constantly compared with
them. Alan reflected: "She was always referred to as my sister. When
we would go to church and people would introduce her, she wouldn't
have her own name—she'd be 'Alan's sister.' "

The expectation of living up to another's reputation can extend
across generations. A PK's family tree frequently reveals a long
tradition of ministers on one or both sides of the family. The pressure
to follow in their footsteps can be great. One egregious example is the
tragic case of Aaron Burr.

THE TRAGIC LIFE OF AARON BURR

Aaron Burr was vice president of the United States under
Thomas Jefferson, but he is probably most widely remembered for the
duel in which he killed his long-time political rival, Alexander
Hamilton. Historians tend to paint Burr as politically inept and
personally roguish. One wonders how his life was affected by his
struggles as a PK and his attempts to find an identity distinct from the
long generations of preachers who preceded him—one of whom was
the renowned theologian and revivalist preacher Jonathan Edwards.

Burr's childhood was filled with tragic losses. His father, Aaron
Burr, Sr., was a Presbyterian minister and the second president of the
institution that became Princeton University. The senior Burr was
frequently absent on church business and appeared to provide more
material than personal support to his family. He died before Aaron's
second birthday. There was no time for mourning, however: Gradua-
tion ceremonies at the college were only two days away, and Aaron's
Uncle Timothy was in the graduating class. Jonathan Edwards,
Aaron's maternal grandfather, was invited to become the college
president. He arrived during a smallpox epidemic, and he died less
than six months later, apparently from complications related to a

vaccination. A few weeks after that, Aaron's mother died. He and his sister were sent to live with their grandmother, who died of dysentery less than six months later. For the next four years, Aaron and his sister were moved from home to home until they eventually became wards of Uncle Timothy.

Surely Burr's case is exceptional in its heaping of tragedy upon tragedy. Any child with such a history would need extraordinary measures of understanding and stability. We do not know whether he received such emotional support. But we may well ask, To what extent did Aaron Burr's heritage as a PK affect his adult life? His grandfather Edwards had himself been heir to the pressures of a family tradition of ministry:

> Edwards felt the burden of great expectations, knew the satisfaction of exceeding them, and eventually paid the heavy price they exacted. . . . The only son of a minister and the grandson on his mother's side of Solomon Stoddard of Northampton, perhaps the most powerful New England clergyman of his time, he was conscious of a long-standing heritage of ministerial vocations. His family situation—surrounded by sisters, influenced by a highly intelligent, willful mother and a demanding father, and considered a likely heir to Stoddard—surely exerted great psychological pressure upon him.[8]

As with his grandfather, Burr's spiritual pedigree was apparently taken for granted. It is likely that the perceived richness of his spiritual heritage tended to eclipse both his struggle for identity and his desire to come to terms with a tragic childhood.

> Burr's anguish was exacerbated by the fact that most considered his ancestors as saintly. Everywhere he went he was forced to hear laudatory words. . . . Everywhere he turned, Burr found reports of the saintliness of his family. Everywhere he went doors opened because of their goodness. Nowhere did anyone mention the foibles. Burr loved his family . . . [but he also] hated them for being unavailable and for deserting him. There was no outside validation for that feeling.[9]

Nor could Burr escape the bind with his peers at college. One historian writes of a religious revival that swept the campus during his college years:

> A number of his classmates experienced conversions, and his friends appealed to him to come to Christ and remember the examples of his blessed parents and grandparents.[10]

Of course, reconstructing the psychological history of a man who died more than 150 years ago can be only a tentative venture at best. What makes this interpretation of Burr's life so compelling, however, is the way the description seems to fit the lives of many ministers' children today. Although most do not endure all the kinds of tragedies that Burr suffered, many have sought therapy because of years of verbal, physical, or even sexual abuse behind the closed doors of the parsonage. Every event, from mild disappointment to trauma, must be integrated into a child's developing sense of self by being explained, discussed, or otherwise dealt with directly. Children left to their own devices to give meaning to their experiences will exaggerate and distort them according to a child's limited point of view. Children need adult help, but for many PKs, the adults themselves are more interested in maintaining their glorious images of the pastor's family than in helping their children through hurts and fears.

All this affects a PK's development of a sense of spiritual identity. Even young children are sometimes expected to be spiritually mature beyond their years, and this can feed their otherwise normal desire to be admired.

■ My earliest recollections of being a minister's son involved feelings of exceptionality. I can remember the congregation covertly and overtly treating me as though I had the means by which to speak directly with God. My youth and ignorance did not allow me to actively dissuade this generalization. I wanted to believe that I was special, that I was somehow "better" than other members of the congregation.

Sooner or later, however, the child is bound to realize that the generalization is based less on an actual relationship to God than on people's expectations.

Furthermore, it is often said that faith can only be "caught, not taught." Much of what the pastor's child learns about faith and relationship to God is not taught from the pulpit, but is caught in the relationship with parents at home. One hopes there will be little discrepancy between the two! But even then, where does the PK go for spiritual counsel? One minister's daughter said, "Struggling to find my own faith seemed an almost impossible task."

■ When your earthly father is your minister, who is the one who's going to teach you about your heavenly father? It's just very, very confusing. You don't know where one ends and the other begins, or how to differentiate them.

By itself and in time, a consistently positive relationship between a PK and understanding, thoughtful parents will resolve this confusion into nothing more than a stopover on the way to spiritual maturity. But where clergy or congregation are hesitant to establish clear boundaries, the PK may find it difficult to distinguish feelings toward parents, the church, and God. One minister's son tried to establish his own boundaries through rebellious behavior:

■ I had such a love-hate relationship with my father and the church. As a child, I think you kind of equate the two. You equate God with your father. So during those early years, and especially during those times of trying to struggle for an identity, it was extremely difficult for me. I rebelled against being a PK.

Thus one difficulty for the PK's spiritual identity is to come to terms with being both the child of a pastor *and* a child of God and over time successfully separating the two. This involvement is not just a child's confusing God with earthly parents, but also a matter of how others perceive and respond to his or her behavior. Some PKs feel that they never get any "credit" for their spiritual growth. Here the problem lies not in the young children's inability to separate their parents from God, but in the inability or the unwillingness of some church members to view the children as separate from their parents, with their own personal relationship to God, commitment, and spiritual identity as individuals.

■ When I went to youth group, people usually thought I went because my dad made me. And when I had a right answer or I had a new idea or insight to share in our youth group, I felt as if people thought I got those ideas from my dad and not my own head.

There is a terrible irony in this. On the one hand, the pastor's children are expected to display exemplary Christian behavior. They should be actively involved in the youth group, and they should know the answers to Bible questions and the like. On the other hand, even when they fulfill these expectations, their motivation and initiative are questioned. The message almost becomes, "You don't have your own spirituality; you just have whatever has spilled over from your father." Jim and Sally Conway offer an example of this:

When one of our daughters was in a time of rapid spiritual growth, she would stand almost every Sunday evening to share something God had been teaching her. A woman eventually said to her, "Well, we can always count on you to have something to say in the sharing time. Your dad must put you up to it."[11]

This woman could have rejoiced with the girl and encouraged her growth. Instead, her spiteful and sarcastic response could only serve to dampen the girl's enthusiasm.

PKs face yet another difficulty in forming a spiritual identity, a problem they share to some extent with their parents. Clergy are expected to be examples of a close and abiding relationship with God, and this expectation is often extended to the children. The problem comes when the type of faith extolled is unrealistic—what has recently been called a "toxic faith," having more to do with religiosity than a living relationship with a gracious God.[12] Everyone experiences both high and low points spiritually. But if both congregation and clergy parents are intolerant of the low points, the pastor's children may receive a double blow: the message from both sides that doubts about God are to be suppressed rather than worked through.

A pastor's daughter expressed the pressure of spiritual expectations and had this recommendation for clergy parents:

> ■ I don't know how they can do it, but they should help their children find out who they are supposed to be, not who the parents want them to be or think they ought to be. You don't have to have this terrible feeling that you're betraying the whole family system if at certain points in time you can't say, "I believe in Jesus Christ," or even understand what that means.

What are PKs to do? How can they cope with the personal and spiritual dimensions of their "identity crisis" in a way that leads to wholeness? To pastor's children these are urgent questions. In my research for this book I encountered many who had toyed with the idea of writing such a volume themselves. A few stated emphatically, "If you don't write the book, then *I will*."

THE DRAMA OF BEING A PK

I see the PK's search for identity as a drama enacted on the stage of the congregational community. Therefore I have structured the book in terms of a metaphor of a dramatic play. This metaphor seems appropriate, for as one pastor's son said, "Part of the problem was that my dad was the pastor, and we were all kind of in the background. We were expected to fill our roles and almost be actors in a play."

The script that defines the role PKs play in this drama is drawn from common stereotypes and expectations. The cast of characters is divided into four groups: the PKs themselves, their parents, their peers inside and outside the church, and the congregation.

Each element of the drama will be considered "ecologically," that is, as parts of a larger whole that work together to form the social environment in which PKs struggle to create a stable sense of identity.

In the final chapter the PKs have the last word and suggest ways in which the drama itself might be rewritten for future generations of ministers' children.

A word is in order regarding the "ecological" approach, as I have used the term here. Few, if any, of the statements in this book can be generalized to include all PKs. Children are born with different characteristics into different families, congregations, and communities. All these factors and more go into the making of a childhood. The point of the ecological way of understanding is to find common factors in the stories of the PKs and then to examine how these factors interact in specific cases. This is much more complicated, of course, than simply saying that being born into a pastor's family is good news or bad news. But that complexity is much closer to the truth.

For this reason the order of the chapters is somewhat arbitrary. Each presents a facet of the social environment, but each is interrelated with the others, and together they make a whole. It is a bit like trying to decide where a circle "starts."

The drama is not the same for every PK. There are important differences in the staging, in the particulars of the script, and in the composition of the cast. Moreover, each element is partially dependent on the others: The stage is set according to the script, but scripts must also be altered for the characteristics of the stage, and the same script will be performed with variations in meaning by different casts. The book must therefore be taken as a unit and can only suggest the outlines of how the life of any particular pastor's child can be understood.

This said, let us begin by taking a look at the stage on which the drama is acted out. Chapter 2 examines the problem of unclear social boundaries in the lives of ministers' children. How do PKs establish a clear sense of who they are when they live in the proverbial glass house?

NOTES

1. Thomas Maeder, *Children of Psychiatrists* (New York: Harper & Row, 1989), 49. Emphasis added.
2. Kathy Cronkite, *On the Edge of the Spotlight* (New York: Morrow, 1981), 17. Emphasis added.
3. Ibid., 18.
4. See, in particular, Erik Erikson, *Childhood and Society* (New York: Norton, 1963), and *Identity: Youth and Crisis* (New York: Norton, 1968).
5. Erikson, *Identity: Youth and Crisis*, 87.
6. Cronkite, *On the Edge of the Spotlight*, 263.
7. Alyene Porter, *Papa Was a Preacher* (New York: Abingdon-Cokesbury, 1944), 17.
8. Edward M. Griffin, *Jonathan Edwards* (Minneapolis: University of Minnesota Press, 1971), 6–7.

9. J. Lee Shneidman and Conalee Levine Shneidman, "Suicide or Murder? The Burr-Hamilton Duel," *Journal of Psychohistory* 8 (1980): 161.

10. Suzanne Geisler, *Jonathan Edwards to Aaron Burr, Jr.: From the Great Awakening to Democratic Politics* (New York: Edwin Mellen, 1981), 108.

11. Jim Conway and Sally Conway, "What Do You Expect from a PK?" *Leadership* 5 (Summer 1984): 84.

12. Stephen Arterburn and Jack Felton, *Toxic Faith: Understanding and Overcoming Religious Addiction* (Nashville: Oliver Nelson, 1991).

PART 1

The Stage

CHAPTER TWO

Growing Up in the Glass House

In a scene from a recent novel, the teenage son of a rural Baptist minister visits his girlfriend, who is home alone. Soon they are in her upstairs bedroom. The boy happens to glance out the window and sees a gossipy neighbor staring back at him from her house—through a pair of binoculars.[1] Fact or fiction? Call it, perhaps, a literary "embellishment," but not an outrageous one. No PK has ever told me of being spied on with binoculars, but many report feeling as if they are under constant surveillance by the congregation.

Living in a "glass house," or having what is commonly known as the "fishbowl syndrome," is the clergy family's unshakable feeling that its every action is being scrutinized by church members.

> ■ I always felt as if we were being watched as a family whenever we were in town or in the church. I was scared to death that if people found out that I or my family wasn't perfect, they wouldn't like my dad or want him to be their preacher anymore.

For some, the feeling of being watched pervades the home, as if the walls were made of glass. Some congregations seem to have an endless curiosity about the minister's family. What kind of marriage does the pastor have? Do the spouses fight? Are the kids obedient, or are they rebellious troublemakers? Some PKs recall only a vague sense of being watched: "Though I can't think of specifics, I remember sometimes feeling as if everybody knew everything about my life." For others, the lack of privacy is more oppressive: "The fishbowl experience played a big part in my life. I just detested the constant exposure."

Scrutiny can be glaring, as illustrated by Jim and Sally Conway:

"Barbara, you didn't have your eyes closed when we were praying. And you're the pastor's daughter!" boomed the Sunday school teacher in front of the entire primary department.

How did she know, our oldest daughter wondered, *unless her eyes were open too?*[2]

And who knows whether binoculars aren't being used from time to time? It is a plausible idea.

■ We had just moved to one church, when a member rang the doorbell to complain that my kid sister had her feet on *their* sofa. The parsonage was set far enough back from the street that a casual glance wouldn't have caught her in this "compromising" position! This was the same church that watched the comings and goings of my boyfriends, knowing what time they left each evening—as if my parents weren't there and thoroughly aware!

The feeling of living in a glass house can be accentuated in small towns or small congregations where, as one PK put it, "every town member seemed to know each other and what was going on." Gossip spreads quickly. There is little anonymity for any member of the clergy family: "Because I lived in a reasonably small town, everyone knew who I was—that my dad was a pastor."

Whatever the setting, the fact is that church members often seem to know more about the life of a pastor's family than they have a right to know. Because most clergy families live in the same community as the congregation, it is easy to learn the latest news on what is happening. Privacy is even rarer for families who live in parsonages. Sometimes parishioners overhear family conversations. Rooms in the house may be used for Sunday school or other church functions. Whereas most kids grow up with a sense of "this is my room," a private place that they fashion to their liking, PKs in parsonages recall having to tidy up their rooms on Saturday so that a Sunday school class could meet there the following morning. Because the parsonage is church property, some people feel free to come and go at will.

To the minister's family, all this suggests a lack of respect for their need for privacy.

■ We used to live in a parsonage that was physically connected by a door to the church. People were always coming in unannounced and meddling in our things—not taking, but using!

Like the parishioner who complained about the PK's putting her feet on "the church's" sofa, church members may casually assume that not just the parsonage, but everything in it is public property. To what extreme does this go?

■ One parsonage we lived in was connected to the church by a breezeway. I often had to clean my room meticulously, especially when we were having an open house or party. We even caught one church member going through our closets during one such open house.

How would we react to finding guests going through our closets? We would regard it as a rank invasion of privacy. Raiding closets might be rare, but less outrageous behavior is just as repugnant for what it represents: a lack of appropriate social boundaries in and around the pastor's family.

APPROPRIATE BOUNDARIES

What are a family's social boundaries?[3] They are the "rules," often unspoken, that we use to define who is part of our family and who is not and how we interact with each other and the outside world. These rules are tied up with a host of expectations and routines that define our family identity and distinguish us from other families. These identity-creating and identity-preserving rules may range from the strictly routine ("We always eat dinner together") to the almost visionary ("We help people in need"). They define the boundaries between the family and the community ("We don't let strangers into the house") and between relationships within the family itself ("Arguments between spouses do not involve the kids").

Families do not live in a vacuum. They cannot make rules that flatly contradict the reality of their social environment. To survive, every family has to "fit" its surroundings, which may mean adjusting expectations. The question is, how much should a family adapt to its environment, and how much should it expect the social environment to adapt to it? The ultimate question for the family's social boundaries is, who has the right to define who we are and what we do?

Privacy. What happens, within vague limits, between members of most nuclear families is considered their business. How parents raise their children is their decision; how children behave is the family's concern, no one else's. But to the PK it may seem that the clergy family's life is everyone's business. Who defines what is private information and what is for public consumption? Imagine the feeling of violation experienced by the PK who wrote, "I have had friends, whom I have talked to and shared my problems with, who then proceeded to tell others in the church." Another PK confided her marital difficulties to a licensed therapist in the congregation, only to find that the counselor had spread the stories around. In this instance, the counselor committed a double violation, betraying both a personal trust and a professional obligation of confidentiality. What justification is there for making this kind of information public property?

Would not we feel intruded upon if someone were simply to walk into our home without warning? True, some families have a kind of "open-door policy" for friends, relatives, or neighbors. Such families are probably less likely to find parsonage life unreasonably intrusive. Others will insist on some advance notice, regardless of who is visiting. But who decides what is an appropriate policy? Do clergy families have a right to insist on privacy, or may church members come into the parsonage as they please on the grounds that it is "their" property? If a family does not live in a parsonage, where does one draw the line?

Boundaries involve how the family interacts with the world and also how family members interact with one another. Every child needs some private psychological "space," the freedom to be an individual, to have his or her wants and needs respected, if not always followed. This need is asserted even in infancy.

Daniel Stern tells of a mother who was playing with her infant daughter. The girl apparently had a low tolerance of physical stimulation and did not react well to the usual games of tickling and making faces. The mother, instead of heeding her baby's response and toning down her play, intensified her efforts. That led to even more rejecting responses from the infant, who closed her eyes and averted her head.[4] This is an early example of boundary violation. To the sensitive observer, the infant's reactions are a clear signal to stop. This mother, however, was oblivious to her baby's need because of her own need to "succeed" at the interaction. Fortunately for all, the girl eventually grew tolerant of her mother's stimulating play, and the negative cycle was broken. Had this not happened, however, the child would have continued to have great difficulty defining personal boundaries with her mother.

Obviously, some parents are poorer than others at allowing their children to set these personal boundaries. A highly intrusive style in parents can contribute to a weak sense of self in children that will persist into adulthood. Children must be allowed private space and even private thoughts. I know of one mother who followed her children everywhere, even into the bathroom, droning on and on in a never-ending monologue. This mother, it seemed, could not allow her children to develop normally and become their own persons; her own identity was so weak that she needed her children to be a part of her.

This is admittedly an extreme case; the point is that all children must deal with the matter of "differentiation" as they mature.

Differentiation. Differentiation, loosely stated, is the task of defining who one is as an individual, a working self-concept that is not unduly controlled by emotional pressure from others.[5] It is also a lifelong process. It entails the freedom to define what is "me" and what is "not me," where my thoughts and feelings end and yours begin.

Children cope with intrusion and the invasion of privacy in different ways. Some give in to the pressure, essentially sacrificing their right to independent selfhood and becoming emotional extensions of their parents. One PK described the emotional fusion with her mother that has persisted even in adulthood:

> ■ The colors I chose for my wedding were my mother's choices, and I realized they were not the best for me at all. And I've had the experience of being in a prayer group with my parents where I literally felt I was almost being absorbed back into her. I sat there feeling I was becoming her. And there will be times I'll look down at my legs, feel my own body, and feel I'm becoming her.

Other children fight tenaciously and may seem unreasonably sensitive to any violation of their desire to decide for themselves.

> ■ The thing that really pushes my buttons is the attempt to curb my freedom in any way, in any area. I'm almost pathological about it. You can't tell me what to do; no one will tell me what to do. . . . I experience immense emotional claustrophobia at the thought of any situation or person having control over my life choices or restricting my freedom of action in any way. After leaving the church, I remember thinking, "No one will ever again tell me how to live my life."

Later on, we will see that the "rebellion" typically expected of PKs can often be explained as a struggle for freedom, to escape restrictive and suffocating rules imposed by anxious parents and congregations. A child who was compliant for years may at some point see an escape and run for it, to the confusion and shock of the family.

The difficulty for many PKs in their struggle for identity is that they often feel more like actors in a play than real people. It can feel as if the part has already been written and the script set, with little tolerance for improvisation. The role expectations can be so rigidly defined that the PKs feel as if they are not allowed thoughts, feelings, or the right to define personal boundaries. It is the difference between feeling loved and respected for *who you are,* as opposed to being loved for *the role you play* in someone else's life.

Balance. In reality, of course, life situations are not so black and white; they are not either-or, but a matter of balance. When a congregation is generally caring and respectful of boundaries, occasional intrusions are not resented.

■ I have never lived in a "fishbowl." I was always sheltered by the home and at church. The congregation are all loving and mature people, so they give people privacy.

■ I think that many people are interested in our family because they care about us as people. Once there was a physical problem in the family, and it seemed that in no time many people knew—and it was something I really wanted everyone to know.

Sometimes a fortuitous combination of the right circumstances with conscious effort frees the minister's child from the feeling of living in a glass house.

■ Even though we are a pastor's family, Dad and Mom never let it get to us. They kept church separated from the home. Also, being mostly in suburban areas meant that physically it wasn't easy for congregation members to watch. Anyhow, we are a fun, pretty good family, so there was little to be embarrassed about.

The fishbowl syndrome is absent here: first, because the parents made an effort not to let church business intrude into the home; second, because the family probably lived at a distance from the church; and third, because there really was little of interest to see! The boundaries seem to have been clearly marked.

BOUNDARY VIOLATIONS

The violation of social boundaries comes in many forms, and there are many boundaries within any social system. Certain kinds of violations seem common to ministers' families. Each clergy family will probably experience some, but not all, the combination helping to create the stage on which the family's life is played out. What follows is a synopsis of some common boundary problems and how they influence a PK's search for identity.

Boundary Violation 1: *Congregations expecting too much of the clergy family's time and energy*

Families are different in how much time they need or want to have together. Yet *all* families need at least some time together, and they like to feel that they have the freedom to determine when this will happen. For most nonclergy families, there is an accepted boundary between work and home life. If work is done at home, it is by choice and not because the job requires it. For many clergy families, however, the demands of the ministry cross the boundary into the home. Having family time without interruption may be difficult, if not impossible. Ministers and their spouses commonly report being overworked and underpaid. Where the church is concerned, they are expected to be at every function, perform every unassigned task, make even the most minor decisions, and be on duty every hour of every day.

■ In situations where someone else could have been consulted, my father was burdened with the problem. Additionally, people would call late at night or on his day off to seek counseling or help of some type. My father was always willing to take care of any situation which arose, but he should not have been expected to be on duty twenty-four hours a day. He needs time off just like anyone else.

The need to compete with a demanding congregation for their parents' time and attention is one of the most common complaints of PKs. Again, celebrities' children have a similar problem, as Kathy Cronkite notes:

Fans appear to feel in some way that they have a right to the time and attention of their idol, and to some extent, they may be justified. . . . [But the] fan's possessiveness is in direct conflict with the child's sense of ownership of his or her parents.[6]

Clergy are dedicated to a life of service, and many demands of church members arise from legitimate needs. Yet the clergy family also has legitimate needs—such as spending time together as a family— that are too often ignored by the church members. Some PKs feel jinxed: Every time the family gets together, something happens in the church that requires the pastor's immediate attention.

■ In the home, it bugged me that we could never do anything as a family without the 95 percent probability of someone calling or coming by, crying their eyes out over something!

Even when the family is on a much-deserved vacation (and some congregations are reluctant to grant even this), the pastor—to his children's consternation—may suddenly be called home to officiate at a funeral.

■ People, I think, have always expected too much from my father. They have expected him to be there every time they needed him, no matter where he was or what he was doing. And even if he hadn't been home long enough all week to sit and catch his breath, they'd still insist on his immediate presence.

In many professions, certain boundaries are recognized and accepted: You don't call me at home or on my day off or on vacation or in the middle of the night. Some clergy would feel guilty setting such restrictions, but nevertheless they must make a conscious effort to maintain clear boundaries somehow for the sake of the family.

■ People would be in and out of our house, interrupting family and meal times, etc. The *telephone* is the worst intruder to a PK's home. We take it off the hook often!

The children see that these demands indicate a lack of respect for their parents' needs and interests:

■ I often thought it was unfair when people would call on my father at all hours of the day and night for help! Or they would expect my mom to organize and play the piano and be present even when interests and talents did not match.

■ When my parents were pastoring one particular church, the people thought my mother was Wonder Woman. She directed the choir, led a women's group, assisted with Bible school, taught a children's group, and so on! It also appeared that everyone would share their problems with her. The problem was, my mother wouldn't have anyone to share her problems with. She would really stress out every few months and get mad at the world.

Sometimes the disregard of boundaries becomes sardonic:

■ I vividly remember being upset when a man would come to our home and sit by my father's bed and tell him his problems, while my father was struggling with an illness.

Intrusions like this take their toll. As we will see later, they can develop an enduring cynicism that leads PKs to avoid the ministry as a vocation at all costs.

■ I made a childhood vow never to marry a minister. How many times have you heard that? I remember one reason I had, and I told my mother, that I didn't want to share my husband with the whole world. I'm not unselfish enough to do that.

This commitment to avoid pastoral ministry may not be reached without a struggle. Many PKs have an earnest desire to serve God, but an equally strong desire to preserve boundaries in a way that their parents did not.

Nevertheless, this is only one side of the story. It is one thing for a PK to feel that the congregation expects too much of the parents, who are viewed essentially as "victims." It is quite another to see the problem as the parents' inability to establish suitable boundaries in the first place.

Boundary Violation 2: *Clergy neglecting to maintain clear boundaries with their congregations*

There is an old saying, Give them an inch, and they'll take a mile. And if you feed a stray kitten one saucer of milk, you had better be prepared to start buying cat food. People can hardly be blamed for wanting more of what seems to be a good thing. Church members who make unfair demands are not likely to change their ways unless the pastor does or says something about it.

Even so, many pastors and their spouses are reluctant to speak up. This reticence may stem in part from confusion over what they have been taught about ministry. Some parents were explicitly taught in seminary that the needs of the church come before the family; and only at great cost, after years of sacrificing themselves and their family relationships, did they change their perspective.

This boundary is often violated another way. Loyalty to the church may not prevent pastors from bad-mouthing church members in front of the children. This raises the question of how and when to express honest emotions. Children are not always prepared to deal with the frustrations of their parents, and they may lack the maturity needed for balanced judgment. Instead of learning something useful about human nature, they may take on their parents' resentments.

> ■ My dad would come home after every staff meeting and pound his fist on the supper table, saying, "Reverend Doe is so bad!" Sometimes he told us the petty power problems people were causing. Of course, it affected my opinion of these people. There were some bad situations, and we understood that some people just caused trouble. . . . In the end, Reverend Doe was temporarily put in an authoritative position and fired many of the staff, including my father. What am I supposed to think about the church?

No doubt this pastor's frustration was legitimate, but did he handle his anger appropriately in front of the children? Consider this incident by way of contrast:

> ■ As we were growing up, Mom and Dad never discussed church members and their problems with us. This particularly included people who had anything against my parents. If we found out, it was by hearing it around the church, and that was seldom. My parents didn't tell us for many reasons: They didn't want us to have negative feelings against any particular church member; they knew we wouldn't be able to control those feelings if we knew; and they wanted us to realize that when someone said or did something "bad," it didn't make that person bad "all the way through." We never, ever had "roast parishioner" for dinner.

This family recognized the problem of venting strong feelings in front of the children and made a conscious effort to teach moderation and maintain a clear boundary between work and home.

The "Messiah Trap." Making a rule never to discuss church business at home is a simplistic solution to the problem of boundaries. Sometimes the effort represents a way to avoid a problem, especially if a minister has weak self-boundaries.

People who can assert appropriate social boundaries do it on the basis of a fundamental, gut-level conviction of their right to do so. This conviction grows out of experiences with other people, primarily their parents, who have respected their individuality. To the extent that they have been deprived of such a foundation, they will lack confidence and self-esteem. The needs of others are legitimate and must be reckoned with, but people must be able to look after their own needs. For some people, service to others grows not from strength, but from weakness; it is the result, not of grace overflowing in their lives, but of a need to be needed. It is the disappointment of living with the illusion that if I am "good" and sacrifice enough, someone will finally treat me with the honor and respect I crave.

This condition, common to many Christians, is what Carmen Berry calls the "Messiah Trap."[7] It is based on the double-edged lie that "If I don't do it, it won't get done" and "Everybody else's needs take priority over mine." A pastor caught in this trap fails to see that he himself is the reason that everyone else expects him to do all the work. Suppose my wife complained that I never pick up my socks, yet continued to pick them up *for me* day after day. When would I ever learn to pick up my own socks? My wife may reap some benefit from seeing herself as the long-suffering and responsible person, but the more important thing is for me to learn to be responsible. Pastors caught in the Messiah Trap need to recognize the absurdity of trying continually to meet the needs of others while running themselves into the ground.

Ministers who have trouble defining and differentiating boundaries probably grew up not having had their personal boundaries respected in childhood. For them, the void created by this condition is too painful to address directly, yet it demands to be filled. They can become preoccupied with the ministry to the point of becoming emotionally unavailable to their families.

Ministering out of a sense of emptiness becomes a treadmill. There is momentary encouragement as sincere Christians applaud the self-sacrifice. But fleeting praise cannot fill the void, so the pastors feel compelled to sacrifice more and more even while the returns diminish.

When PKs are young, they may accept their parents' lack of boundaries as others do: as exemplary Christian living, a model of selfless giving. As the children grow older, however, they may see the situation in a different light, as this embittered pastor's son did:

> ■ As a kid, I saw it as Christlike, as if he were a sacrificial person. He sacrificed, he suffered, and I admired that. But when I grew up, I started to get tired of it. In my late teens, I was old enough to put two and two together. When I went away to college and got some distance from my family, I started to see that it wasn't so much that Dad was being Christlike as much as that he was not dealing with his own issues. . . . You don't do something because you feel guilty about it; you do it out of love. *A healthy person says no when feeling intruded upon, and Christ doesn't hate you for that. It has taken me years to get that into my head* (emphasis added).

Only with time and distance did this PK learn that his father's suffering was caused not only by unreasonable church members, but also by an inability to set proper boundaries by saying no when it was appropriate.

Creating Confusion. Parents who have trouble maintaining boundaries create confusion for their children. Does ministry mean you have to do whatever the members of the church want you to do? Where does one draw the line? A pastor's daughter encountered this dilemma:

> ■ My mother has a very hard time setting boundaries. We were talking about how men in church can be intrusive. There are men in church who want a kiss from me, and I don't want to give them a kiss, but it's that "obligation kiss." And I've actually thought to myself, "Well, I'll go ahead and give him a kiss because he writes huge checks to the church." There are men who try to get a little "touchy-feely," and that's gross, but that's the way it goes.

To this point the PK was following the "party line." In time, however, she attempted to define her own boundaries:

> ■ But now I've put a stop to that. A handshake—that's as far as it goes. And my mother said that you kind of have to give them a kiss. I said, "Mom, for God's sake, if you don't want to give them a kiss, don't! Stick your hand out—that's as far as it goes. You don't need to have people intrude on you like that." She said, "Well, but you know—you just kind of have to sometimes. It would be rude not to." I thought, "That's sick; that's really sick."

No matter how intrusive the congregation, clergy parents bear some responsibility for keeping appropriate personal boundaries.

Pastors' children judge faith and service by what they see in their parents' lives. If their parents can model clear boundaries, the PKs are less likely to feel that their spiritual identity is at odds with their personal identity or that personal boundaries are somehow un-Christian. But for some pastors and their spouses, taking responsibility will entail painful soul-searching and a reassessment of their heart for ministry.

Boundary Violation 3: *Letting the demands of the pastor's professional role and image contaminate the parent-child relationship*

When violations 1 and 2 converge, they lead to a third boundary violation for PKs. Pastors having weak boundaries and confronting high congregational expectations feel pressure to abdicate parental authority and let church members dictate the children's behavior. This violation expresses itself in several ways.

Image. To some PKs, it seems that image is everything. Clergy parents may coach their children on how to make a certain impression with the congregation and then bask in the praise that results from their obedience. "What a good little girl!" or "What a good little boy!" become words of affirmation for the parents. The children, however, are not blind to this:

> ■ Growing up, everyone knew who I was, always having to sit in the front, and sit nice, and sit happy, and if need be, play the piano. My dad made sure my piano teacher taught me hymns so that I could play them once in a while at church, so I could become the church pianist. It was a way to make him look good.

This is the confession of a girl who has been used, made a means to an end, offered up as a way for her father to obtain the praise he wanted without appearing to ask for it. The result is a sense of abandonment.

Children do, of course, help to form a family's public image. Other parents, not just pastors, are concerned that their children make good impressions in how they look and act. Responsible parents will train their children in the behavior that is proper for their environment. The question is, for whose benefit is the training?

Who Benefits? It is appropriate to train children so that they fit in socially. It is also appropriate for parents to communicate their moral convictions and, with them, a sense of how their identity as a family relates to their rules of behavior. It is quite another thing, however, for the parents to give training motivated by a wish to avoid conflict or embarrassment. For one minister's son, the matter of "image" intruded into his relationship with his father:

> ■ I remember one time pulling a prank at school. For my father— I think this is part of the pastoral psyche that he went through—it was so important what other people thought. The teacher called him and told him what I had done. And he got so embarrassed. I can remember so vividly, he came home, and I can picture him almost like a mountain lion, just pouncing on me. He was fairly liberal with the belt. And the things that he said still stick out in my mind. *It wasn't so much what I had done; it was what people thought* (emphasis added).

The punishment for this PK was administered, not in proportion to the misdeed, but in proportion to the father's anger over being publicly embarrassed. The important issue for the father was not what he himself thought, but what everyone else would think. It is as if he became an extension of the group.

Therein lies the betrayal: the feeling that the pastor-father had let public opinion determine his behavior instead of making up his own mind. In this, he abandoned his role as a full partner in a father-son relationship.

This experience can bring a depersonalizing feeling. The boundary guarding the father's reputation—his relationship with his public—was stronger than the one that protected his relationship with his son.

Sermon Illustrations. Pastors may be unaware that using stories about their children as sermon illustrations violates their privacy. An episode from the parsonage may be cute sermon material for the pastor, but an embarrassing public revelation for the PK. Occasionally PKs hear stories from their childhood for the first time from the pulpit, and this takes them by surprise. Who reaps the benefit? Pulpit illustrations from a preacher's family life are often gratuitous, used for effect rather than content. Is using them worth the PK's potential embarrassment? Does the PK have a right to be consulted first?

There is a need for balance. Recognizing boundaries does not mean that all sermon illustrations focused on PKs are taboo. But exposing a child's life in a cavalier manner indicates a lack of respect for the personal boundaries.

Unwilling Recruits. Another kind of violation occurs when clergy parents who have problems maintaining appropriate boundaries routinely find themselves emotionally exhausted, with nowhere to turn for solace—nowhere, that is, except to their children. Some pastors who become compliant "messiahs" before the congregation may relate to their children the same way. An inability to maintain healthy boundaries in the face of congregational expectations may lead to inappropriately expecting the children to make up the lack, thus violating their boundaries. One pastor's daughter described how her family's boundary problems passed from one generation to the next:

> ■ I take on people's problems, which my father did too. And in order to get any sense of approval from him, I had to listen to his problems, too. That is what makes me who I am in some ways, someone who is interested in listening to people—though lately I have noticed that I don't want to hear anyone's problems. I've had enough, years of problem-listening. I'm ready for you to listen to my problems! Sometimes I wish I could send a little bill—my therapy bill—to my father . . . pay up!

This pastor, needing the congregation's approval, took on their problems to gain it. At home his daughter was recruited to do the same for him. Note the confusion of identity: She views herself as genuinely interested in others' problems, though she realizes that somehow this violates her personal boundaries. Who listens to her problems? A therapist, to whom she must pay a fee. She feels it is an injustice that her father should have been the one to counsel her, not the other way around. No wonder she feels he ought to pay up for services rendered!

Boundary Violation 4: *Idolizing the clergy family*

As we saw earlier, some congregations seem to have an endless fascination with the pastor's family. Family arguments are especially titillating.

> ■ Some people who may have overheard a family argument or some trouble talked about it. Some people also feel as though they have the right to know what goes on in your private life.

> ■ If there was a relationship breakup and it involved one of the PKs, it became the gossip of the church. If two members of the family were arguing, many of the church members knew about it.

It is not always clear how church members come by the information, but once they do, the gossip can spread like wildfire, sometimes coming back to the clergy family in hurtful ways.

> ■ One year our family had a great deal of difficulty with one of our close relatives. My parents were arguing about it. Privately! Someone in the church found out and said my parents were getting a divorce. Divorce had never been mentioned. The matter between my parents was settled in a couple of days, and they love

one another more now than ever. The people in the church caused a lot of trouble by exaggerating.

It is not surprising that the gossip often focuses on the pastor's children. Whom they date is of particular interest:

■ When I started dating girls, I found out that a lot of the time the news spread very quickly. Because I'm a PK, people are watching. At times I was just dating and didn't feel we were really serious. But people were already talking about it; people already knew.

Consider this girl's dilemma:

■ My boyfriend, Paul, and I have been together for several months. He lives in Central City. There happens to be a church member who lives in a town near there. We walked into church on Sunday, and this church member, the usher, said to Paul—without my even saying, "This is my boyfriend, Paul"—"You must be the guy who lives in Central City." Paul goes to church once, and somehow it's known. People have asked me, "Are you marrying Paul? Do you have a ring yet? Where's the ring? When's the wedding? How many kids are you going to have?" Is it any of your business? No!

Sometimes the PK has the feeling that more than curiosity is involved:

■ When I was seen with a guy, most of the congregation would want to know "what was up" between us, and sometimes I felt as if they wanted the right of approval.

The attitude of church members seemed to be that this girl "belonged" to the church because her family represented the church. She was everyone's concern.

There is another side to this violation. Sometimes the congregation is on the lookout for faults and failures.

■ In a small town where you are known by most, people like to look at what you're doing and be curious, in a way seeing if you'll make a mistake. People tended to talk about the family, especially us kids. If any of us got into any mischief, in or out of the church, everybody knew about it.

■ People were always watching me. If I messed up, they would jump on that mistake, always quick to point it out. I felt a lot of guilt about my Christian witness because it seemed I had no room for mistakes.

A Double Standard. PKs resent being singled out in this way, especially since it often implies a double standard. That is, people may be quick to criticize the actions of the minister's child, but ignore similar or worse behavior from other youth in the congregation.

■ I felt that if I did something considered wrong by the congregation, they all found out. My actions were blown out of proportion. For example, if I was at a party drunk, the people all thought how terrible that the pastor's kid drank. However, if any other kid in our church did the exact same thing, it was no big deal. That never seemed fair to me. In fact, most people never found out about the other kids who were with me!

The lack of fairness can push PKs toward rebellion:

■ The people in my church were legit about their Christian faith—but their kids got away with *MURDER!* I remember them jumping on Sunday school tables, climbing on the roof—all that kind of thing—while I got in trouble for wearing too much makeup! It made me really bitter, and I overcompensated by smoking and drinking. . . . Even if *they* didn't know, *I* was rebelling against perfection!

Why the curiosity, the scrutiny, and the double standard? As other writers have observed, clergy families fulfill an important symbolic function in the congregation. William Douglas calls this phenomenon the "royal family": the clergy family are the symbolic parents of the congregation and represent that extended family to God and the community.[8] They are therefore expected to be models to the flock. They should exemplify Christian life in every aspect, especially family relationships. Church members are very likely to pattern themselves after what they see in the pastor's family:

■ People in the church would model their personal lives on us, and to do so, they had to study us. One couple even had the same amount of children as our family and would repeat the phrases Dad used for discipline and so on.

If church members want to know how to rear children properly, they have only to look to the clergy family:

■ I felt that my parents set the trends for proper parental guidelines for families with children my age. Wearing pants to church was acceptable only after I wore pants to church. Wearing a bikini was okay after my mother bought me one. Going to a school dance was okay only after my parents gave me the okay.

Thomas Maeder tells a similar story:

"All the mothers kept a close watch on my daughter's clothes," one minister's wife told me. "If she went to school in a skirt that was above the knee, they figured it meant that God had okayed shorter skirts this year."[9]

Mythmaking. The pastor's family is idolized and looked up to as the epitome of Christian living. Each member is expected to be "more" of everything morally desirable: wiser, more spiritual, more forgiving, more self-sacrificial. Clergy should have ideal marriages and well-behaved, spiritually mature children. Some church members even expect PKs to be able to offer spiritual counsel to them, as if they were extensions of their parents.

Many myths have some basis in fact: Clergy may have better marriages by and large, and their children may indeed be better behaved than others. The myth is that the image persists regardless of the facts, because it expresses a wish that it should be so. Most adolescents belong to a fan club of one kind or another because teen culture by its very nature nurtures popular idols. The teenagers may dream of meeting their idol face to face and imagine how wonderful that person would be. When the teens discover that the object of their worship is really just an ordinary human being, they react in one of two ways—either by denying the report to keep the myth alive or by angrily rejecting the idol for dispelling their fantasies.

So it is with clergy families. But the myth has a double edge and cuts two ways. Even as church members look up to the clergy family for inspiration, they also are alert for slips and stumbles—anything that tarnishes the image.

> ■ I always feel people are watching our family and seeing what we do, our behavior. They seem to watch and wait for problems or trouble in the family, and they seem to be pleased when there are problems. In a way, I get the feeling sometimes that many people, especially people my age in the church, are wanting our family to fail.

Why would church members want the family to fail? The truth is, we often have a great deal of ambivalence toward our heroes. On the one hand, they represent what we would like to be. We build them up and are vicariously reassured by their goodness, gaining a sense of "virtue by association." On the other hand, living next to someone so perfect must ultimately remind us of our shortcomings. To the extent that we wish to avoid dealing with our faults, we will emphasize the faults of others. We take pleasure in discovering that our heroes have feet of clay because seeing faults in someone who is supposed to be better keeps us from feeling bad about ourselves.

> ■ Certain members of the congregation, whose own families were in disorder, were jealous of us and tried to highlight even the slightest mistakes. They also blamed my dad for their own spiritual weaknesses.

People may avoid dealing with their problems or taking responsibility for their spiritual growth by picking on the pastor's family.

■ People scrutinize pastors' families and pick up on any fault. I think that because they feel their family and children should be like the pastor's, when they see a rift they can be very critical.

This kind of scrutiny creates a great deal of confusion for the pastor's family, especially if they have begun to believe they really are better. The problem is, how a congregation responds to the clergy family only partially depends on how the family behaves. Partly to blame is the congregation's need for the family to fulfill a certain role. Performers are sharply aware of the fickleness of their fans and of the precarious nature of public success. Kathy Cronkite quotes Nora Davis, the daughter of actors Ruby Dee and Ossie Davis:

So many people become successful and don't understand why. . . . They have no idea why people adore them, and they don't wish to be adored like that after a while. Then they're afraid if they deviate at all, they'll fail. They're not themselves anymore. They're whatever it was going to take to be *out there*.[10]

Compare this with the recollection of a minister's son:

■ My father tried his best not to disappoint anyone. He complained and raved at home but smiled at church. My mother became and still is extremely paranoid, reading things into many of the church members' words and comments.

Success, whether in the performing arts or in the pastorate, is not based only—or even primarily—on sheer talent. It is a function of being able to please. This is an unstable base at best. For those whose self-concept is closely tied to success, there is a lack of security, a fear of failure, even paranoia. Even for those whose self-images are more secure, maintaining success may require compromising one's identity. Fans are fickle. How much should we give to stay in their good graces? It is like staking our career on how well we play a certain role, and then agreeing to take on the role—without seeing the script in advance! Recall what one PK said at the beginning of the chapter: "I was scared to death that if people found out that I or my family wasn't perfect, they wouldn't like my dad or want him to be their preacher anymore." Having to be perfect for a congregation is a suffocating role, especially for children who are still trying to figure out what is okay or not okay. The expectation is based on a congregation's need to have someone be perfect for them, or a pastor's wish to be perfect (Boundary Violation 2), or both. This expectation is further legitimized by a mistaken notion of Christian modeling that leaves no room for grace.

Modeling Grace. I have described this phenomenon as "idolizing" for a reason. When congregations look to the pastor's family to be perfect, it is idolatry. When clergy families expect this of themselves, that too is idolatry. Why? Because the church becomes preoccupied with the minister's family, instead of focusing on the Lord, who is the center of their life together. Churches should not preoccupy themselves with looking for "good" behavior in clergy families, for there is only One who is good, and all other human goodness has its source in him (Matt. 19:17). Clergy families must be models for their congregations. But what they are to model is a realistic and abiding relationship with God and the awareness of a daily need for his grace.

In churches where grace is a reality in everyday relationships, people are encouraged to discover their spiritual gifts and the special places they fill in God's service. In this environment there is mutual support, acceptance, and a respect for boundaries. There is an understanding that all who attend the church are human, including the clergy family, and this humanness alone does not disqualify anyone from ministry. Ministers' children are not forced into identical molds, but allowed to develop individual personalities in a context of love and understanding.

Boundary Violation 5: *Making clergy responsible for their children's actions, and PKs responsible for their parents' actions*

How any children behave is to some extent an indicator of how they have been reared by their parents—but only to an extent. Many other factors influence a child's personality or behavior, including innate temperament, peer groups, and accidents of history. Parents may carry a large share of responsibility for how their children turn out, but they can take neither all the credit nor all the blame.

Parents tend to forget this, however, especially if their self-esteem relies significantly on how their children turn out. A further complication for clergy parents is the common expectation that PKs will be model children (Boundary Violation 4). Violation 5 is in part a circular reinforcement of that: Clergy parents are judged as inadequate and deficient if their children are not perfect. Rather than recognizing this myth for what it is, church members may criticize the parents, or the clergy may unjustifiably criticize themselves. Either way, the pressure put on clergy parents is tremendous.

■ There was a time when my mother came home from church, and she was ready to cry. The deacon's wife wouldn't speak to her all day Sunday, and we knew it had a lot to do with our short dresses and the way we wanted to wear our hair and our face, and they didn't want us to.

Even when clergy try to maintain appropriate boundaries between their professional and parental roles, the pressure persists:

> ■ My parents were supposed to have perfect Christian kids. We are all Christians; however, I was definitely far from perfect in their eyes. If I behaved in a way not approved of, it must be my parents' fault. I think they felt very pressured by this. Since Dad was a PK too, he helped me deal with society's expectations a lot. My mom struggled more to allow us kids to grow up "normal" and experiment like other kids. I think most of the church's expectations centered on how well we kids modeled Mom and Dad's Christian lifestyle.

The Roots of Rebellion. Can the congregation judge the parents' Christian lifestyle on other terms? According to psychoanalyst D. W. Winnicott, there is a broad range of parenting that can be considered "good enough."[11] To expect perfection of any parent and to insist on perfect children is both unrealistic and unreasonable. It is symptomatic of treating the children as extensions of their parents and not as persons in their own right.

There is a great irony in this expectation, especially where so-called rebellious PKs are concerned. Much rebellious behavior is rooted in efforts, either conscious or unconscious, to be recognized as an individual. Ministers' children will sometimes go to great lengths to show that they do not have to be what everyone expects them to be. Often the rebellion is more against role expectations than directly against the parents, to whom the youth still feel allegiance. But the strategy backfires: Instead of recognizing the PK's individuality, the parishioners blame the parents, which only reinforces the feeling the children wanted to escape. Then both the children and the parents are in trouble, and everyone feels worse than ever.

But PKs and other children in the congregation can also be made to suffer for their parents' decisions and prejudices. The story of Romeo and Juliet is a classic example of how feuds between adults can destroy the lives of their children. In the church setting, children are often dragged along as their parents take sides in congregational splits. People who take issue with the pastor feel they must take issue with the PKs as well, even if the children have not contributed to the conflict. The failure to separate the adults' interests from the children's can cause painful rifts in the latter's friendships.

> ■ The children who were my friends in the church obviously had parents. The parents were involved in the argument, and the

parents made the children take sides. If one of my friends' parents decided to take a side opposite from the one my dad was on, that meant I couldn't hang out with my friend anymore. I think that's so wrong. The church was split fifty-fifty. One friend's parents were on one side, but he started dating a girl on the other side. So he didn't want to be with me anymore.

It is ironic that the PK's friend could declare independence from his parents by dating a girl from the opposite side of the split, but somehow could not maintain his friendship with the PK.

Developing a sense of individuality entails having a sense of responsibility for one's actions. It is not helpful to blame clergy parents continually for everything a PK does in deviation from perfection. Ministers' children are not extensions of their parents; they should be allowed and encouraged to grow into a relationship of mutual accountability.

Boundary Violation 6: *"Triangling" PKs into conflicts that have nothing to do with them*

The final example of boundary violation involves what family therapist Murray Bowen called "triangling." Simply put, triangling is a way for two people who lack the ability to stand up for their own beliefs to avoid a conflict. Instead of dealing directly with each other, they involve a third party, who either becomes a go-between or provides a mutual annoyance for the sake of distraction.

Ministers' children occasionally find themselves being drawn into conflicts between their parents and members of the church. Clergy parents are usually concerned to keep children out of the fray, except perhaps for some ranting and raving around the home. Some church members will try to ensnare the children because either they have failed to achieve their goals or they do not want to confront the pastor directly. They try to enlist the PK's "help" or sympathy, often by complaining to them about their parents. One PK reported that church members would make "small snide remarks about Mom and Dad and their problems." Another wrote:

■ Parishioners would ask pointed questions of a naive me, discuss criticisms in front of me, and attack me because they wanted to strike at my parents.

It is unfair to allow conflicts with the pastor to involve the children. This type of triangling is a corollary to Violation 5, in which children are made to bear the consequences of feuds between adults. But triangling is more than a failure to view the children as separate people;

there is an ulterior motive, namely, to get to the parents through the children:

> ■ Church members have drawn me in by advising me to persuade my parents one way or another. They would just say something mean about my parents to me.

Ministers' children who are triangled this way feel the discomfort of being caught in the middle, and they may try to persuade the church member to talk directly with the parents:

> ■ Church members have tried to pull me into conflicts with my parents on a couple of occasions. They try to have me get at my dad or mom for them, or make nasty remarks about them to me! They never can talk to my parents about their conflicts. Instead they want to make me a kind of "go-between." This is unfair! I would never do this to my parents, and I have told them many times to talk with my parents. But they still try their old tricks, until you get stern with them.

It is unfortunate that PKs are placed in situations where they have to "get stern" with parishioners. Some realize that the go-between ploy violates Christ's exhortation to resolve our differences one-to-one (Matt. 18:15). We must also see that triangling PKs is but one more way to treat them as a means to an end, as tools instead of people. If we have differences with the pastor, it is between us and the pastor alone—the children should not be manipulated to become disloyal to their parents.

Pastors must not allow their children to be dragged into conflicts through triangling. And PKs themselves must learn to say no, sometimes with sternness, but always in the recognition that maintaining proper boundaries is better for all concerned.

A COMPLICATED ENVIRONMENT

All in all, the social environment in which a PK grows up can be enormously complicated. Erikson's model of psychosocial development assumes a gradually expanding sphere of relationships, from the mother-child relationship in infancy out to the family, to school, and so on. The formation of identity in adolescence is an attempt to integrate what has been learned and experienced about self and others in each of these contexts. But a PK's world is generally more densely populated than that of his peers. Moreover, it is not always clear what role all these people do or should play in the PK's life.

Families can usually provide a relatively private haven for children to develop their identities gradually. Yet this becomes more

---

Boundary Violations

1. Congregations expecting too much of the clergy family's time and energy

2. Clergy neglecting to maintain clear boundaries with their congregations

3. Letting the demands of the pastor's professional role and image contaminate the parent-child relationship

4. Idolizing the clergy family

5. Making clergy responsible for their children's actions, and PKs responsible for their parents' actions

6. "Triangling" PKs into conflicts that have nothing to do with them

---

difficult when people press in from all sides with a dizzying array of emotions, expectations, and ideas. When the boundaries in and around the family are unclear, no one is quite certain which voices to listen to or which leads to follow. This is what it means to grow up in a glass house, amid the watchful eyes and clamoring voices of an insensitive congregation competing for attention.

One pastor's daughter wrote to me after reading an article of mine about PKs. Her letter gave eloquent expression to the variety of emotions that spring up in congregational life. Her words make a fitting conclusion to this chapter.

■ There are times when I think of my childhood, especially as I focus on my family life, and I realize my memory is crowded with what seems like hordes of people. What I observe now is I as a child observing all of them: taking them in, being interested in them, feeling frightened by them, feeling loved by them, feeling admired by them, feeling sorry for them, feeling crowded by them. The result of this inundation is mixed: I have known many interesting and good people, I like many different kinds of people, and I think I am good at empathizing and understanding others. On the other hand, I also have struggled intensely to develop and maintain my own personal boundaries in a social context. I believe I was so immersed in others that my own self was difficult to define and communicate.

NOTES

1. Terry Pringle, *The Preacher's Boy* (Chapel Hill, N.C.: Algonquin, 1988).

2. Jim and Sally Conway, "What Do You Expect from a PK?" *Leadership* 5 (Summer 1984): 84.

3. A parallel discussion can be found in Cameron Lee and Jack Balswick, *Life in a Glass House* (Grand Rapids: Zondervan, 1989). See especially chapter 3, "A Family Within a Family."

4. Daniel Stern, *The First Relationship: Infant and Mother* (Cambridge: Harvard University Press, 1977): 110–14.

5. Murray Bowen, *Family Therapy in Clinical Practice* (New York: Jason Aronson, 1978). The concept figures prominently in Lee and Balswick, *Life in a Glass House.*

6. Kathy Cronkite, *On the Edge of the Spotlight* (New York: Morrow, 1981), 192.

7. See Carmen Renee Berry, *When Helping You Is Hurting Me: Escaping the Messiah Trap* (San Francisco: Harper & Row, 1988); and Carmen Renee Berry and Mark Lloyd Taylor, *Loving Yourself as Your Neighbor* (San Francisco: HarperCollins, 1990).

8. William Douglas, "Minister and Wife: Growth in Relationship," *Pastoral Psychology 12* (December 1961): 38.

9. Thomas Maeder, *Children of Psychiatrists* (New York: Harper & Row, 1989), 50.

10. Cronkite, *On the Edge of the Spotlight,* 150.

11. See D. W. Winnicott, *The Maturational Processes and the Facilitating Environment* (New York: International Universities Press, 1965). See also Bruno Bettelheim, *A Good Enough Parent* (New York: Alfred A. Knopf, 1988).

CHAPTER THREE

Speaking the Truth in Love?

Chapter 2 concluded with this pastor's daughter's lament: "I was so immersed in others that my own self was difficult to define and communicate." In building personal identity, definition and communication are two sides of a single coin.

Identity is both an individual and a corporate matter. Like all other children, PKs need to define identities that make sense in their social context. As tentative identities take shape, personal boundaries must be communicated to others, who must in turn validate them— and so on in a cycle of mutual affirmation. Good communication helps this development, for it is the avenue by which children receive adult guidance and feedback. To the extent that communication with key adults is distorted or blocked, children will have to make sense of their world with only the limited tools and experiences of a child.

"Speaking the truth in love" is the catalyst by which churches develop spiritually (Eph. 4:14–16) and people mature psychologically. Many church members manifest God's grace responsibly in their relationships to one another. Open communication is valued in a context of mutual trust. Even when they fear the truth, the people accept it as requisite for growth.

Unfortunately, in some churches there are barriers to plain speaking. In chapter 2 we saw how clergy families are frequently idolized by their congregations. Often this is a symptom of a still broader idolizing tendency: an unrealistic "triumphalism," a kind of Christianity that views pain and negative emotions as part of the sinful past Christians are to leave behind. It is, after all, easier to deny that emotions like rage and fear have any place in a Christian's life than it is to deal with them. Through denial the church hopes to maintain a one-dimensional kind of spirituality that requires a superhuman, if not perfect, pastor.

MYTHS THAT PERSIST

Two interrelated myths are generally found in churches that have the idolizing tendency. The first, already discussed in chapter 2, is that all members of the clergy family must be model Christians, ideal examples of an unwavering faith and a joyous marriage and family life. The myth survives not only among church members, but sometimes among the clergy themselves, who may even support it from the pulpit. One PK became angry when her father, citing in a sermon her mother's rather serious illness, suggested that neither spouse was the slightest bit anxious about it. The PK remembers thinking that her father's impenetrable calm could only alienate those in the congregation who honestly struggled with problems of their own. She reflected, "We weren't raised to think that we were part of the human race."

The second myth, which feeds on unclear boundary conditions, is the belief that if the pastor's family fails, the church will automatically fail also:

> ■ My vision as a child was that if the pastor's family came down, the rest of the church came down. It all starts with a lie that says, "We must keep it together because if we don't keep it together, then the people in the church can't keep it together."

It is as if the clergy family must be spiritual *on behalf of* the congregation. As long as the lie persists, church members will not get too concerned if their own spirituality is flagging. When the myth is dispelled, the foundation of this vicarious faith is undercut and the congregation feels threatened. Small wonder, then, that some church members are concerned that the pastor's family be perfect! In implicit and explicit ways the congregation communicates to the family, "Don't let us down."

> ■ I was in extreme pain, but it felt such a betrayal to verbalize that to anyone because it seemed I had such wonderful parents. We're all from such wonderful Christian families. So what do you do with all this garbage? You just stuff it.

Should this supposed transference of spirituality fail, there is still one more defensive strategy for the church members: Place all the blame on the pastor and get rid of him. "I've seen a lot of churches crucify their pastors," said one minister's son, "because they confessed their faults and admitted their weaknesses. The congregations drove them away."

We see from these myths that in this social context only the positive, the good, the triumphant are affirmed. Anger, sadness, pain, and fear are treated as aberrations, to be either denied or prayed out of existence. Love becomes grace-less, redefined as a superficial togetherness or the absence of conflict. Instead of allowing faith and prayer to be the means of opening their hearts to God, pain and all, church members become slaves to the need to rid themselves of whatever threatens the image of the serene Christian.

To protect the status quo, church members adopt rules of communication about what can or cannot be said and what feelings are or are not acceptable to express. These rules of communication are seldom conscious or explicit. Watch how young children begin to put words together in sentences, how they form plurals and tenses. Parents do not need to teach the rules of grammar explicitly: The children pick them up by "conversing" with adults. Even when they are old enough to form correct sentences, the children would be unable to explain how they learned to do this or even what all the rules are. For that matter, neither could the adults who have "taught" them! The rules have been both taught and learned implicitly in the course of daily interaction.

Similarly, rules of communication may be taught and enforced by a social group, such as a family or a church, in ways that may not be directly conscious to the members. In what Lyman Wynne called a "pseudo-mutual" family, for example, anything that threatens their superficial sense of togetherness is ruled out.[1] Negative emotions and differences of opinion are frowned upon or punished outright. Family members share the myth that they are close and caring, and this belief becomes a procrustean bed in which all perceptions and feelings to the contrary are cut off, denied, or distorted to fit. The myth so controls the family communication that it gains the status of an absolute commandment.

■ In our family, there's no system in place to deal with conflict. That's what was really terrifying for me to realize: "Thou shalt not have negative feelings."

Dealing with Negative Emotions

Developing a stable and healthy identity requires that we integrate both the pleasant and the unpleasant experiences of life. No one's life is all ups and no downs, all happiness and no sadness. Children become angry, frustrated, and irritable, and so do adults.

The difference is that adults already have an array of mechanisms in place to deal with these emotions, while children are still learning.

Adults are sometimes threatened by the undiluted strength of children's emotions. A frustrated or angry boy might shout, "I wish you were dead!" How parents respond to such an outburst depends on how comfortable they are with their own anger. Some will respond empathically and help the boy acknowledge and resolve his feelings. But others will feel their own emotions getting out of control and react accordingly. One parent might respond with denial: "You don't mean that!" (Yes, he does!) Another might use an outright prohibition: "How dare you speak to me in that way!" (What about the way you are speaking to him?)

What does the child learn? He is feeling rage and communicates that to his parents in a primitive yet natural way. But what he learns from the interaction are rules about feelings and the communication of feelings. The parent who responds with denial is essentially saying, "Don't have that feeling," and in that prohibition is making a rule.

But the underlying reality is that the tone of the response also implies rejection. Because the reality of the feeling is undeniable to the child, it is only one short step from "*my feelings* are not acceptable" to "*I* am not acceptable." One PK described his parents' intolerance of his negative feelings and its effect on his sense of self:

> ■ I interpreted all of that as it was not okay to be me. I don't know who "me" was, but whoever "me" was, it was not okay to be me. And I realize now just how much negative stuff I had. I was just a powder keg of repressed anger. Even now I feel that my parents are impatient with my pain. I've shared some of this with them, and it's as if they say, "Come on, hurry up, get healed, get rid of all this." But they still don't know what to do with it.

Negative and hurtful emotions must be realistically incorporated into a healthy sense of identity. Many families attempt to exclude these with implicit rules of communication. Christian families that maintain a lopsided triumphalism find religious justification for this. Again, the PK may feel the pain with double force because the injunctions that serve to maintain the myths are supported by both the family and the congregation.

Honest Communication

In my research, many PKs reported that negative feelings were handled both in the home and in the church with direct and open communication. The negative emotions were worked through with love and prayer.

■ Negative feelings are always dealt with head-on. Talking things out is the only way to handle such feelings. A lot of prayer and honesty is the only way to go!

This PK's parents were intentional about resolving conflicts, thereby setting a positive example for the children:

■ When my mom got angry or upset, my dad was always the person who calmed her down. When they disagreed, they didn't hide it from us. Instead they worked out the problem right there, which gave us a great example to follow. A verse that my parents valued between them was "Don't let the sun go down on your anger." My parents always tried hard to resolve any problems before we went to bed.

In some families this intentionality is embodied in a regular family ritual:

■ In our family, we had weekly council meetings in which much was discussed, including negative emotions. We were encouraged to share negative emotions whenever we had them with the hope of working them out.

Both at home and at the church, much depends on a pastor's willingness to get to the heart of a matter and resolve differences promptly.

■ Dad challenges people to confess these emotions, to give them up to God and deal with them. He doesn't ignore the negative emotions in people, and he believes they should be dealt with, not suppressed.

A pastor's daughter wrote:

■ Negative feelings were always dealt with. My father hates to ignore problems; he deals with things up front and honestly. He wanted to know how we were feeling. I always took my problems to him. In the church, he handled problems the same way. If he had a run-in with a person or felt there were hard feelings between him and another, he wouldn't let those feelings build up, but would go to that person and talk it out.

It is significant that this person was able to say, "I always took my problems to him." She felt that her father was genuinely interested in her feelings and therefore that he cared for her. Moreover, she saw that her father was consistent in how he handled problems at home and in church. The same is true for the PK who wrote:

■ I was allowed to be "mad, sad, cranky, obnoxious," because my parents taught me that everybody needs to be that way once in a while, and they modeled that consistently.

Even with open communication about feelings, different families have different styles. Some accentuate the positive:

■ We were taught to address the problems and talk about them. We were also taught to try to look at the positive things and support one another in love.

Other families use a somewhat more analytic approach, as with the PKs who wrote, "Negative emotions were handled by sorting through the heart of the problem and then discussing it rationally" and "We tried and still try to deal with negative emotions by trying to see where they are coming from and why." Understanding the source of one's emotional reactions gives a sense of perspective and can be useful for the future. Incidentally, accepting and being empathic with a child's negative feelings does not mean that parents give up the responsibility to set limits:

■ Good communication in our family dealt with negative emotions: If correction was due, it was given, but likewise comfort, support, etc. In the church it was the same—Mom and Dad dealt with the problems themselves.

Open communication can be difficult at home among the people who are closest to us. But the important thing is that children feel accepted as they are:

■ Negative emotions in the church were handled with a little more tolerance than in my home—we were expected and raised to be positive about life, although we were accepted unconditionally with or without bad attitudes. In the church, negative emotions were handled very gently and carefully.

Suppressing Negative Emotions

Some clergy families seem intolerant of negative emotions or disagreements and consciously or unconsciously impose strict rules to suppress them. In these situations there is little or no support for open communication about feelings. One PK put it simply: "We were made to feel that negative emotions were *wrong.*" Another wrote:

■ Negative emotions in my family were usually suppressed. I did not grow up in a very communicative family. We were not too open and honest. I did not feel comfortable sharing intimately with either my father or my mother. My sister was my closest confidante, but she too was fairly distant.

Prohibitions may be so strong that they cannot be broken even in the face of obvious and serious consequences:

■ Our family is totally dysfunctional. We never communicated. All emotion, good and bad, was tenuous or repressed if ever expressed. Even with my mother's nervous breakdowns, we still can't communicate!

As there are different styles for keeping the lines of communication open, so there are different ways to keep them closed. Some families and churches operate somewhat passively according to a rule that one PK described this way: "Negative emotions were submerged and not talked out—stiff upper lip." With others, bad feelings are dealt with more actively. Sermons are a favorite device, not only in the pulpit, but at home: "We would get a long talk from Dad about how we should think." Some pastors act swiftly to suppress outbreaks of emotion: "Dad came down hard on negative emotions both in our family and in the church."

Like these pastors' families, many churches are not comfortable with negative emotions. One PK observed a common pattern in one congregation over a span of twenty years:

■ The congregation was and is still handling problems in a hypocritical and dysfunctional fashion. They don't fight fair and are usually divided!

Problems can be denied or covered up. One PK wrote, "Our denomination really has a tradition of masking feelings, whether they are positive or negative." Still another said, "In the church negative emotions were often brushed over in the hope they would disappear."

A common observation is that congregations resort to gossip instead of dealing with conflicts directly. Unfortunately, avoidance— whether through denial or gossip—is only a temporary solution. Emotions are submerged or brushed aside only to reemerge later. Pastors' children may then witness loud and hurtful disruptions in the church:

■ People tend to gossip and go behind people's backs to complain. Occasionally people express negative feelings in public, but usually in a way in which they make fools of themselves by being abusive or unjustified—but they usually don't realize it. They rarely go to someone to discuss their complaints.

■ Negative emotions were usually kept under wraps until they eventually exploded and gave everybody a lot of grief. In the church there were often negative undercurrents between social groups, or so-and-so didn't like him or her or them. The feelings weren't handled well.

In our positive examples we saw the pastor intervening effectively to confront negative emotions and work through them. The intervention must not come too late, after the damage is done. Damage control is not the best motivation for intervention:

> ■ Negative emotions were dealt with quickly, perhaps superficially at times. My parents worked toward positive feelings in the churches they served and were hard on the people who tried to upset the fruitbasket.

By contrast, acting quickly from a sense of urgency entails risks also. The urgency may derive from a need to maintain the status quo rather than a desire to heal relationships authentically.

Thus many PKs grow up in environments where negative feelings are poorly tolerated and not handled constructively. When people are not allowed to express confusion or disappointments openly, they are very likely to bottle them up or withdraw into themselves. They may recognize the negativity but see no one to help them sort it out or understand it. The contradictions can be extremely confusing to a young mind:

> ■ I saw the results of anger everywhere, in my family and in the church. The church felt anger was wrong, yet the parishioners could be very judgmental, critical, and incredibly vicious. It was a dilemma for me while growing up.

Left to themselves with this jumble of impressions, PKs may come to the wrong conclusions about the emotions they see, even feeling false guilt.

> ■ PKs tend to know a lot about people, especially negative things, and this knowledge, combined with an injunction to silence to protect the privacy of everyone in the congregation except one's own, is a sure formula for guilt. I have seen more than I should have about people, have known my parents' frailties, while at the same time protecting them from the mean intolerance and judgment of others, have felt the hurts of others before I was able to protect myself from believing their pain was my own. This knowledge and awareness has been trapped inside of me, and my greatest relief has been in simply being able to speak firmly and clearly about what I have seen and known and felt. That process of speaking is easily interrupted, however, particularly by guilt.

This girl needed her parents' help to establish clear self-boundaries, to know whose feelings are whose, and who bears responsibility for those feelings. As she points out, speaking the truth helps clarify the line between what we feel inside and what we see outside.

For another girl, the best way she found to keep her trapped thoughts inside was to enter into a "conspiracy" with God:

> ■ During my time growing up, I often would think, "My dad has it all wrong," but I couldn't let him know that; I couldn't argue with him. It was too scary; it was not acceptable. I got slapped if I spoke my mind, said no about something, or disagreed. So I was very compliant. Inside, I had my own little thoughts, my own little world. I wasn't mad at God, but I think I had this collusion with God. God and I had this nice little relationship. I would run to my room and have a nice little talk with God or Jesus, and say, "We know that Dad's wrong." So I had a lot of anger toward my father, but it wasn't until I was married that I was able to work through that and admit that I had a bad childhood, that I was depressed a lot. Of course, nobody would have known that.

Some adults cannot tolerate the truth.

"Impervious" Parents

If speaking the truth is needed, it must be done in love. Merely venting negative emotions is not a solution if reconciliation is not the goal. One clergy family routinely flailed the congregation at home:

> ■ We had family gripe sessions. After every service we would air all the frustrations of the day. Things said to us were talked about, and so on. It was never planned. The bad thing is that we dwelt on them. Many years and churches later, we were still hashing over the old hurts. All the negative lives on.

This family did not have a rule against *expressing* frustration, but it appears they had one against *resolving* it. To some people, avoiding direct resolution of conflicts seems to be the Christian thing to do. Negative feelings, in the words of one PK, can be "put out by a lot of talking and convincing that they are not of God." Another recalled how his mother rationalized the pain she felt over not dealing with marital tensions:

> ■ The positive message of "stand on the Word and you'll be all right" was taken to extremes and came to mean that people can't be vulnerable.

Spiritualizing problems to make them go away can become oppressive. It can be a symptom of what Theodore Lidz has called "imperviousness," or " a parent's inability to feel or hear the child's emotional needs." According to Lidz,

> The parent may listen but does not seem to hear. . . . These parents cannot consider anything that does not fit in with their own self-protecting systems.[2]

The impervious pastor reinterprets his daughter's pain back to her as *her* spiritual weakness:

> ■ He denies that he has done anything wrong or that he has caused any pain, and he tells us that our problem is that we have gotten away from the Lord. If we can just stay away from the psychiatrists who are feeding us evil thoughts and get back to Jesus, we will know that what we are doing to him, trying to get him to face his behavior and its effect, is sin.

There may be any number of reasons behind closed communication in a clergy family. One is background:

> ■ At home, feelings tended to be suppressed. I do not think that this was only because our family was in ministry. Our dad had a rough family background, and this was more a reflection of that.

Another is the attempt to protect the pastor's reputation and support the idolizing myth. For PKs to freely express themselves in these situations is tantamount to a betrayal of the family.

> ■ We put on this wonderful smile, and everything looked so good. And we dare, dare not let anybody know the pain we have next door, or we would be ruining God's purpose in the church. My father would lose his reputation. There's this little code of ethics that says, "Don't tell the truth" or "Don't reveal."

A Conspiracy of Silence

Both the clergy family and the church have something invested in their myths and the rules of "don't tell" that support them. The result may be a mutual, albeit unspoken agreement to preserve both the myths and the rules.

This denial extends to the way church members view their own children. One pastor's son said his peers in the youth group did the same things teenagers outside the church were doing: smoking marijuana, experimenting with hard drugs, getting drunk in bars, and having a variety of sexual contacts, even at youth group functions. What did the parents think? The PK felt the parents didn't really want to know:

> ■ It's the whole idea of "not in my backyard, not in my community. Not these kids—not these nice, church-going kids. It's everybody else; it's out there." No, it's right here—it's right in front of you!

Little wonder, then, that PKs such as this girl learn denial:

> ■ I would go to church and be all smiles, and greet everybody. I'm not trying to be fake, but I can be that way, knowing that I've just

rolled out of bed and pushed one of the church members out the door. If these people had any inkling of it, they'd probably fall over in their pews. But if I told them, they wouldn't want to know it because I don't do that kind of thing. I'm not that kind of girl.

So a silent contract is signed: PKs and clergy families will keep their feelings to themselves. Under pain of rejection, they are not to disclose their struggles to the congregation. Negative emotions, arguments, disagreements—all become terrible secrets for the family to protect. Some PKs are fairly bursting with the wish for somebody to know the truth:

■ In high school, I remember—I guess this is normal for an adolescent—going to my room and just sobbing, "Why was I born?" I thought, "Wouldn't the church just *love* to hear. . . ." I even taped a family conversation because somehow I wanted everyone to realize how we were always yelling at each other. Then the phone would ring and my mother would pick it up, and her voice would change just like that and become melodious: "Hello!" Everything was fine, and we were all quiet as mice while she was on the phone.

The injunction to silence is as likely to be implicit as explicit.

■ You go through various struggles in the family, and there's always that tendency to try to keep things quiet, keep things within the core of the family, and not let the rest of the body know. It hasn't been until recently, at least as far as I'm concerned, that we've seen people more willing to talk about their problems, about their past, their hurts, their sins. To divulge those things, when I was a child, just wasn't done. You didn't share that part of your life with people.

Many PKs learn to play the role well, allowing their parents to look like the models everyone seems to want:

■ At home, Mom and Dad were as negative as any other parents. At church, they never shouted or displayed anger, etc. But this wasn't necessarily hypocritical, since we usually acted like little saints, leaving little for them to get angry about—except for those times when we would hear, "I'll deal with you when we get home," muttered under a parent's breath.

Masking the Truth

Far from speaking the truth, some PKs in their pain become masters at deceiving people into thinking that everything is fine. Hiding behind a mask is a way of keeping church members and their expectations at arm's length. It forms a highly artificial self-boundary that protects the real person from outside intrusions.

■ You would never know me: I could let you see this face, or that face, whatever you wanted. What do you want to see of me? I'll show it to you. That was the façade—but the real me was in pain.

Then there is the fear of being found out, the fear that someday their faces might betray their true feelings: "I was afraid of anybody discovering who I really was. I suppose I was never real with anyone." Eventually the masks themselves take on a reality of their own, and it becomes difficult for the PK to have any authentic relationships at all:

■ Until I met my wife and some of my close friends in college, I never really knew how to be in a relationship because I had many façades.

How bad does a problem have to be to get noticed?

■ I had a breakdown when I was younger. I didn't go to a doctor; I never really discussed it with my parents. I certainly didn't go to a counselor. It was just too terrifying to me to admit that I was having a problem. Ministers' children are not supposed to have problems like this. They're supposed to be perfect. I had anxiety attacks; I would wake up in the morning trembling or sweating. And I realize how much I was just kind of going through the motions and trying to pretend to me and everybody else that I was living a normal life.

How could a teenager go through such a crisis without showing at least some outward signs of her suffering? And if there were that much suffering, why didn't anyone notice? The reason is that it was assumed in the church and the parsonage that everything was all right. In varying degrees we bend our perceptions to fit our assumptions. We see what we want to see regardless of the truth.

■ People perceive me, so they tell me, as a gifted, talented person, and I have experienced constant self-doubt for as long as I have been conscious of my feelings.

Another PK summed up the situation in one simple sentence: "My biggest problem was that nobody thought I had any problems."

The unfortunate result of continually masking the truth is that in the minister's eyes, a PK's problems take a back seat to the congregation's.

■ At home, it seems to me as though our needs aren't dealt with as being as important as those of the church, and I don't feel as though he has as much time for us as he does the church.

■ I think we get so engrossed in ministry and in caring for people that for years we put a lot of our needs aside. We put a lot of our feelings aside.

But clergy families must examine the real reasons for ordering priorities this way and assess the cost of doing so. Yes, the ministry requires much physical and emotional energy, and devoted ministers may have to set aside personal needs occasionally to serve others. But perpetually failing to deal with one's needs and feelings as a way of life is neither honest nor beneficial. It is easy to slide almost imperceptibly from engaging in heartfelt ministry into living out the myth of the superhuman, superspiritual clergy family. Once having embraced that lifestyle, a person will not escape it easily.

Adults in ministry must realize that as adults they have already spent years working on personal identity. If their identities are relatively secure, they may be able to constrain their emotions if this serves an immediate, valid purpose. Such constraint is seldom advisable, though people can perhaps do this if need be without suffering long-term consequences.

But is it appropriate to expect a PK to act the same way? The injunction "Don't rock the boat" may have quite a different meaning for PKs than it does for their parents. The parents may interpret this as meaning, "We know we're right, and so-and-so is just being unreasonable for the moment. Let's quit while we're ahead and not create any more trouble than we have to." But the children may interpret the message as "Your feelings in this matter are not acceptable" or "If you say what you really feel, you will get everyone upset." Sensitive children will further interpret the message as an expression of personal rejection.

However clergy parents decide to handle emotions and conflicts in the church, they must at least make the home a safe place where their children are free to express their feelings. PKs should not have to live out the myths that support an unrealistic mode of Christianity; to do so, they will have to deny or push away an entire aspect of their experience. These troublesome feelings do not simply vanish; they may emerge later, bringing confusion to self-identity in adolescence or creating difficulties in adult relationships.

If PKs want to talk, will anyone listen? Or is there an implicit rule in the family or congregation that prevents a hearing? For PKs to develop healthy and well-integrated identities, the best rule of communication for the clergy home is to learn to speak the truth, and to speak it in love.

NOTES

1. Lyman C. Wynne, Irving M. Ryckoff, Juliana Day, and Stanley I. Hirsch, "Pseudo-Mutuality in the Family Relations of Schizophrenics," *Psychiatry* 21 (1958): 205–20.

2. Theodore Lidz, Alice Cornelison, Dorothy Terry Carlson, and Stephen Fleck, "Intrafamilial Environment of the Schizophrenic Patient: The Transmission of Irrationality," *Archives of Neurology and Psychiatry* 79 (1958): 305–16.

PART 2

The Script

CHAPTER FOUR

Little Rebels or Little Saints?

In part 1 we examined the "stage," or the social context, upon which PKs play out their search for identity. Every child grows up in a particular social environment. Each environment in turn has its social and personal boundaries as well as rules of communication that define and maintain these boundaries. Taken together, the notions of boundaries and communication rules comprise one way of understanding the context of human development.

We saw in chapter 2 the importance of clearly defined interpersonal boundaries. Some clergy families seem to have an implicit understanding of this, refusing, for example, to live in a parsonage, where boundaries can become unclear and are frequently violated.

In chapter 3 we looked at rules about communicating feelings both in the minister's family and in the church. The rule of speaking the truth in love means that young PKs are allowed to express their emotions. In so doing, they are encouraged to work out their feelings and understand the feelings of others. Unfortunately, rules of communication can also be used to support a boundary-violating status quo. When this happens, PKs are denied the privilege of expressing or even acknowledging certain feelings, and they must therefore deny one aspect of their existence as they try to formulate personal identity.

Thus the stage is set: Boundaries and communication patterns form the context and backdrop for the development of a PK's identity. In part 2 we will study the "script" that defines what it means to be a minister's child. This chapter looks at some prevalent stereotypes regarding PKs. Chapter 5 extends this study to other expectations that families and congregations place on ministers' children.

STEREOTYPES—PRO AND CON

What is a stereotype? Webster's Ninth gives us this definition: "a standardized mental picture that is held in common by members of a group and that represents an oversimplified opinion, affective attitude, or uncritical judgment."

Now, there is nothing wrong per se with having a "standardized mental picture" if it has a firm basis in fact and experience. For example, my wife and I live in the inland regions of Southern California, and our parents live in the San Francisco Bay area. The climates are very different. On our last summer excursion to visit our families, my wife packed some warm clothing for us, even though the weather was hot around our home. My wife knew that it would probably be misty and cold in the mornings, and she was right.

When we left the Bay Area a week later to return home, we dressed in shorts, even though it was foggy and cold as we got into the car. We would be driving through the flat central valley region of the state, and our mental picture was that it would be sunny and dry there. Again, we were right. We had said goodbye to our parents in the middle of July in foggy weather with the temperature at fifty-five degrees. Four hours and two hundred miles later, we stopped for lunch in ninety-degree sunshine.

Life is much too complicated to meet every day as a completely new experience. We have to order our experiences into mental pictures, concepts, attitudes, and opinions. If we didn't, we would not be able to use past experience to benefit the present (and we would have to pack three times as much luggage).

Stereotypes have their origin in tnis need to simplify. They are seldom purely figments of imagination, but rather have some basis in fact. Yet stereotypes are usually more than simplifications: They are uncritical oversimplifications. They are particularly problematic when applied to people. True, sometimes people can be as predictable as the weather. But the weather doesn't object or get its feelings hurt when you predict incorrectly and pack the wrong clothes! People do not like to be simplified, boxed in, categorized, or labeled. Tell people that you know how they will respond in certain situations, and they are likely to do just the opposite.

Pastors' children often find themselves put in mental boxes. On first encounters with new acquaintances, they are treated like anyone else. And why not? After all, ministers' kids don't wear badges that say, "I'm a PK; I'm different." But it seems that as soon as they are identified as ministers' children, the other person's attitude changes: perhaps to guardedness, sometimes to curiosity. Frequently the conversation turns to satisfying the other's curiosity about what it is like to be a PK and whether he or she fits a certain stereotype.

The stereotypes seem to divide into two jarringly different images: perfectly behaved saints and defiant rebels. Ministers' children disagree on the appropriateness of these stereotypes. One of them stated flatly, "All PKs can fit into one or the other." Another PK made what seems to be a more balanced judgment:

> ■ I have encountered such stereotypical explanations and find it hard to think that PKs can be divided into extremes of trouble-makers or saints without there being mention of the "average" PK. It may be that this belief is propagated because if PKs are either of these personality extremes, they "stick out" more than an average church member and thus are more obvious.

The stereotypes persist whether or not they have validity. Is there any truth in them? Alan Bayer and his colleagues tried to answer this question more than twenty years ago through a large-scale study that piggybacked on a survey conducted by the American Council of Education in 1969. A quarter of a million freshmen entering 390 colleges were asked to complete an information form. More than two thousand of these freshmen were PKs, and their responses were compared with those of the rest of the group. The purpose of the study was to find out if the stereotypes of PKs had any basis in fact. This is how they perceived the stereotypes prior to the research:

> [PKs] are academically superior and highly motivated to achieve. Their upbringing is supposed to have given them firm moral values and a commitment to serve mankind. They are regarded as taking a liberal and humanitarian outlook, being concerned with social problems, and having an optimistic attitude about their solution. In addition, it is assumed that many PKs are, to some degree, rebels against their parents and that this rebellion is manifested in a tendency to reject the religion they were raised in and to indulge in "wild" behavior. Another bit of the folklore is that PKs are social outcasts, isolated from their peers.[1]

What the researchers found, overall, was little or no support for the negative stereotype, but fairly strong support for the positive one. On the one hand, PKs were actually less likely than other freshmen either to have rejected religion or to have left the church they grew up in. They were also less likely to drink, smoke, or stay up all night than students who were not PKs. On the other hand, PKs had higher grades and better study habits; more of their financial support came from scholarships; they were more involved in extracurricular activities; they were more likely to have participated in state or regional speech and debate contests; and they were more likely to be presidents of student organizations. The researchers also found that ministers' children aspired to higher degrees and careers that emphasized social responsibility and altruistic values.

The results of that study should be viewed by pastors as good news. All else being equal, being a PK is not an automatic sentence to a life of misery and psychological maladjustment! Indeed, the results seem to indicate that there are advantages to being a PK. I am not aware of any other study of this scale that has been completed since that one, but if one were to be done now, I would expect the results to be similar.

How, then, do we reconcile this finding with the negative stereotype? As we shall see, the "PK as rebel" is not just an imaginative creation, but definitely has a basis in fact. The key lies in the easily overlooked phrase "all else being equal." If PKs are treated like everyone else, given the same chances, allowed the same freedoms, spared any more intrusive expectations than the next person—under these conditions, the advantages of being a PK will far outweigh the disadvantages.

In my survey, many PKs reported that they had never encountered either the saint or the rebel stereotype. Here are a few of their responses:

■ I'm not really stereotyped at all. They treat me like a normal church member, which I am.

■ I haven't really been stereotyped. I think that people just see you as you are.

■ I never felt any such stereotypes. I never felt any pressure to be anything but real. At church, I've always been accepted for me, not for my parents.

■ I was normally treated like any other kid. I could do almost everything other kids did. I never had anyone keep tabs on me to see if I was rebellious or a saint.

■ I don't ever recall feeling I was a victim of stereotyping. I was not a rebellious child and teen, but instead tried to do what was right and not always go along with the crowd.

■ I have never really been a victim of stereotyping. I just did the best that I could in everything. For the most part, the congregations that my dad has served have respected me for who I am.

Note the common themes in the statements. These PKs feel recognized as individuals in their own right, not as extensions of their parents. They are treated as church members, nothing more; there is no double standard. In short, their boundaries are respected.

ARE PKS LITTLE SAINTS?

But the absence of stereotyping is not universal. We have seen that many congregations have expectations of sainthood for the entire clergy family. For every PK who escaped stereotyping, my survey turned up one who has suffered from it.

■ Lots of people think you're a little saint. Some people find out you're not and try to make you into one.

■ Everyone expects you are more spiritual, inhumanly immune to temptation, knowing the Bible back to front.

Another PK, who couldn't remember specific instances of stereotyping, nevertheless felt the pressure:

■ It's hard to illustrate, but there always seemed to be an underlying pressure to be a saint.

Moreover, it is not just the congregation, but also the parents who impose a standard of sainthood:

■ My father expects me to be absolutely perfect in every way, forcing Christianity onto me. The people in the church expect me to be a saint also.

■ I am expected to do everything right all the time. Sometimes Dad makes me feel like that too. For instance, he makes me go to youth group and church every single week. Even though I want to, sometimes I want a break—as when I have heaps of homework. If I do something wrong, people can't believe it. That is stupid.

By contrast, the positive stereotype can make peer relationships awkward. Again, everything seems to go well at first. Then comes the crucial revelation: "Oh, your dad's a minister?" In some cases, the reaction is mild: a raised eyebrow or a slight expression of puzzlement that the PK does not fit the mental image:

■ I attended a Christian rock concert and was listening and dancing to one of the songs by one of the bands. I was talking with friends and somehow made the comment that I was a PK. One guy said, "You don't act like one."

At other times the information creates a rift. Friends' perceptions change, and the relationships change with them:

■ When we first moved to California, we attended a church near our home. This church had a lot of kids my age, and it was fun at first. Then everyone learned that my father was a minister looking for a new church to minister in, and I couldn't be me. I had to walk, talk, look, and breathe perfectly.

Peers may become self-conscious in the presence of PKs:

■ Peers of mine who swore would apologize repeatedly if they ever swore in front of me. No one ever expected that I too might swear occasionally. I was the perfect PK in their minds.

Perhaps the biggest breach, however, comes when a friend's parents make unfortunate comparisons. Demanding, "Why don't you be like so-and-so," who happens to be a PK, is a sure way for so-and-so to get on her friend's bad side. The situation can bring embarrassment:

■ The worst is to be stereotyped by your peers, or worse yet, as an example to them. The most humiliating example of this to me was when I was at a friend's house one day helping her family move. Her grandmother (also from the church) reprimanded her for not being more helpful and said, "Why can't you be more like the pastor's daughter? She's being so sweet." I felt like melting through the floor!

PKs' friends may actively resent the comparison:

■ I've found that parents are the ones who expected me to be a "little saint." I've often had some of my peers complain to me because their parents compared them with me. Sometimes my friends resented me in that aspect. I have also been referred to as "Miss Perfect" or a "Goody Two-Shoes."

There may be more substantive reasons for rifts developing between PKs and their friends. The PKs are expected to be especially mature and may be unfairly put in positions of responsibility vis-à-vis their peers:

■ In Sunday school classes, if the teacher had to leave the room for a minute, I was always the one put in charge of the other students.

Of course, it is difficult to be just "one of the kids" when you are in charge of the group!

PKs may find themselves continually reminded of the expectations of sainthood, sometimes expressed in public ways. William Hulme tells this story:

I know of one parsonage family who were determined these stereotypes would not affect their children. They talked things over with the congregation, and all seemed to understand. One day, however, one of the children, along with others, got into some trouble at school. In reprimanding the students, the principal (who was not a member of the congregation) said to their child, "The others I can understand, but you, a minister's child, I don't understand." The mother was furious when she heard about this. "When it's not the congregation," she said, "it's the public school. How do you get away from these pressures?"[2]

... OR LITTLE REBELS?

What about the negative stereotype, the PK as rebel? This image, too, seems woven into the expectations of the public. Sometimes the stereotype appears in very subtle ways, as one PK, now a clergy wife, recalls:

- Actually, I never encountered it, but our kids have. People comment on how nice, considerate, well-behaved, etc., they are— "not like most PKs"!

At other times, the expression of the stereotype is quite clear and direct:

- After kids our age found out we were PKs, they would respond by saying, "Gosh, I'm surprised you aren't really rebellious or little hellions. Usually preachers' kids are."

- People have asked me why I am still a Christian when most PKs are really rebellious, causing their parents a lot of heartache.

- The old saying goes, "The two worst types of kids are both PKs: policemen's kids and pastors' kids." I suppose I tried to keep up with the stereotype. I can't remember how many times that was said to me by individuals in the church.

As with the positive stereotype, the negative stereotype interferes with relationships because people see the image rather than the person:

- It seems as if everyone in the church has already placed us PKs in the "troublemaker" category. It's hard to get away from that and develop relationships with these people after I've grown up, just because I'm "guilty by association" to them.

Even in the best of situations, having people continually superimposing stereotypes on you can create some identity confusion. A pastor's daughter who in general is very enthusiastic about her family and life in the church describes the kind of disorientation that being subjected to stereotypes can create:

- It's funny how people say, "Oh, you're a PK! Watch out!" They treat me as if I'm some sort of rebel without a cause, and I'm saying, "Hey, I'm normal! I'm okay!" That's a comment that people have thrown at me every once in a while, and I just think, "Why? Don't you know me?" I feel, "You don't know me if

you're saying that. You think I'm just a wild woman, but I'm
not." And that made me wonder, What is a PK supposed to be
like? Am I weird? Am I abnormal?

A No-Win Situation

It is even more confusing that some PKs are subjected to *both*
stereotypes—by different people, at different times, or in different
places:

■ The biggest conflict is that many people within a church cannot
decide which stereotype to give you. To one lady you're
considered an angel; to a gentleman you are considered a hellion.

Being subjected to both stereotypes is a no-win situation. One
PK made an interesting distinction: The positive stereotype was
encountered primarily outside the church, while the negative stereotype was encountered inside.

■ It seemed as if whenever I was outspoken at church or youth
group, the adults would make comments like, "Well, you know
preachers' kids!" I often found myself wondering, "No, I *don't*
know preachers' kids. Tell me what *you* know!" In public school,
however, I was more or less expected to be perfect. So Christians
expected rebellion, and non-Christians expected perfection.

Another minister's child supports the distinction. In the church she
was automatically blamed for things she didn't do, whereas outside the
church she was expected to be blameless:

■ I encountered both stereotypes. The kids at school expected me
to be a saint, and the people at our own church expected me to be
a troublemaker. The kids at school would say things like, "We
can't say or do that around her" or "I thought you were a
Christian." The people in the church would blame me for broken
objects or misplaced things. For example, there was a problem
with a stove in the church, and an elder came to me and said,
"You really shouldn't play with the stove."

By contrast, as we have seen, some churches expect PKs to be
saints, and their peers expect them to be rebels. So much for
stereotypes of stereotypes!

GETTING BEYOND THE STEREOTYPES

Figuring out which stereotype is "true" or "more true" is not
very helpful when we try to understand pastors' children because most
PKs surely fall somewhere in between. For our purposes, it is more
useful to consider how these stereotypes are born and maintained and

what they have to teach us about a PK's quest for identity. I believe that, here again, the notion of boundaries is the key to understanding.

On the one hand, we must recall the public nature of the PK's life. People with celebrity status are not judged according to the same criteria as everyone else. What may be an unremarkable event in one person's life becomes celebrity gossip in another's. Alyene Porter comments:

> Perhaps we fitted into the timeworn pattern cut to make us the worst children in town. But [all children] have impulses; and since preachers' children spend three-fourths of their time in church, those impulses have to be expressed there and observed by the greatest number of people.[3]

The point seems to be that the actions of PKs are more noteworthy because they are more visible. Anything that a celebrity does is news.

On the other hand, it is just as important to see the situation the other way around: The actions of celebrities and PKs are looked at more closely because of their status. Pastors' children are members of the "royal family," representatives of the congregation, and emblems of the Christian religion. The public scrutinizes those who are seen as representatives. A similar observation has been made by S. L. Carson about the children of U.S. presidents:

> [These] children also were supposed to be the symbols of the nation's ideal of first families. Often they had to live a lie, and, at tender ages before the world, had to grow up in the pitiless glare of the public eye where every failure would be magnified, every success attributed to their father's influence, not their own abilities. And their rage had to be especially suppressed "for the good of the country."[4]

Does this sound familiar? Carson's statement could just as well describe pastors' children as presidents'.

Stereotypes, it appears, do not arise simply from the behavior of ministers' children. The pressure of certain expectations precedes the behavior, and the stereotypes are reinforced by what PKs actually do.

So there is both a positive stereotype—an expectation of sainthood—and the plain fact that many PKs are very well behaved. The expectation may support the behavior. PKs may behave well because it is expected of them and because they fear the consequences to themselves and their families if they do not behave well. Good behavior in turn reinforces the stereotype, seemingly justifying the expectation.

This self-perpetuating cycle can become a trap. First, no credit is given for good behavior because it is only what is expected. As one PK said, "I felt as if I could only do good things because I was expected to, not because I wanted to."

It is simply not true that ministers' children make good decisions because they cannot do otherwise. If their parents have taught them limits and morals, can they not at least be applauded for learning their lessons well and putting them into practice? This refusal to recognize a PK's independent will is a violation of boundaries: treating him or her as an extension of the parents. If ministers' children are not credited with their own decisions—even good decisions—how can they integrate a sense of goodness into their identities?

Second, once the cycle is begun, it is difficult to break. If PKs are acting as little saints, why should clergy parents or congregations think of their stereotypes as unreasonable? If the pastor's children behave well today, don't we have the right to assume they will tomorrow and the next day? Conversely, the children themselves, having played the role for some time, feel they have a reputation to live up to. Their fear of rejection may cause them to be compliant, pleasant, and religious on the outside, no matter how they feel inside.

This trap, the thesis of the saintly PK, is a factor in the creation of its antithesis. Stereotypes are like boxes, and people resist being put in them.

How do PKs escape the trap? Often, through rebellion:

■ I was expected to be "good and always do the right thing." I rebelled to show the church that they could not fit me into a stereotype.

In attempting to break out of the box, PKs may exhibit the kind of behavior that supports the negative stereotype. This negative view, in turn, can be used to the disadvantage of other PKs:

■ I had a party once, and one friend, trying to convince her parents to let her come, mentioned I was a PK. This worked in the wrong way because they said, "That doesn't mean a thing; ministers' kids are probably the worst." Some, in an effort to get away from stereotypes, have created another.

Many people expect teenagers to go through some stage of rebellion, but not all teenagers do so. Many PKs believe they would have rebelled equally as much or as little even if they had not been raised in a clergy home. Others quite adamantly ascribe their rebellious behavior to their struggle to prove the stereotypes wrong, to be recognized as individuals, and to establish an identity less dependent on the expectations of others.

It is not the rebellion in itself that makes PKs unique, for other teenagers rebel for similar reasons. But the irony is striking: Pastors' kids rebel against the restrictiveness of an idealistic stereotype, only to lay the groundwork for an equally intrusive and opposite one.

The term *rebellion* is relative. Many clergy children would describe themselves as having been rebellious at one point or another, but further questioning reveals a very broad range of behaviors under that rubric. Some PKs, on entering adolescence, begin to harbor private thoughts about not wanting to go to church or have silent disagreements with their parents. Outwardly, however, they remain compliant. This is the extent of their "rebellion." Others take this a step further: They remain the well-behaved PK when others are watching, but lead a second, secret life. A pastor's son confesses:

■ I have been classed as a little saint, when really I am not. I would put on a good act while they were around, and then when they left, I would talk and do things behind their backs.

Another PK writes:

■ Church members would be shocked and totally disillusioned if they knew I listened to non-Christian music, went out to night clubs while at school, and spent most of my time with my secular friends.

Still another adds that the behavior was intended to make a point:

■ I wanted to prove a point and resist being put in a "saint's box."

One daughter created her second life when she left home and had an environment in which she wasn't immediately known as a PK:

■ I almost became two completely different people. I was still the perfect daughter and the believer. I went to live in another town and took a job there, my first job. I would go to discotheques at night on my own—things that I know are just a crazy thing to do. But all of that life was hidden. My parents, of course, didn't meet any of my boyfriends. They wouldn't have approved of them anyhow.

Another led her double life while she was still living with her unsuspecting parents:

■ My sister and I both rebelled. She did it in more underhanded ways; she would go out drinking and really get drunk. I went out with boys a lot; I would sneak out at night. I felt I was being wicked by doing it: I had this whole life of my own my parents didn't know about. That was really acting out my frustration.

Still one step further are the PKs whose so-called rebellious behavior is out in the open. One young man, tired of living out the positive stereotype, decided to do something about it:

■ I was always expected to be the chaplain in clubs and groups, give an opening prayer or sermon on youth Sunday, etc. I always responded with a yes. At college, PKs were known to be troublemakers. I drank beer, smoked cigarettes, and snuck out of the dorm—not to be a troublemaker, but to show I wasn't a goody-goody.

The stereotypes of rebel and saint, then, are not simply equal and opposite. Some PKs fit one stereotype, some the other, and some fit neither. The stereotypes are not born of generalizations of how some ministers' children happen to behave, although such generalizations might reinforce them. There is, rather, a logical connection between the stereotypes. The positive image comes first, based on the projected wishes of congregations and clergy families alike. The negative stereotype primarily derives from some PKs' reaction to feeling forced into this idealistic mold.

Some pastors' children have sought to identify a fork in the road in their personality development, when they set themselves in the direction of either rebellion or compliance:

■ I think most of my PK/MK [missionary kid] friends have either passed through a major "rebellious troublemaker" phase or are still in it. Maybe this is because we are expected or required to be "saints"; some give in to expectations; others rebel against them.

■ I think every PK rebels to some extent. You're raised in this pattern, in this category—you're labeled. At some point you have to decide if you're going to be that or somebody else. I don't think that there's any way around that. PKs have to decide what they're going to be. Are they going to go on and follow their parents into the ministry, as a lot of PKs do? But a lot of them rebel and decide they don't want to have anything to do with the church. The two extremes seem to be pretty common among the people that I've talked to.

So PKs may rebel in the service of defining their own identities, much as other teenagers do. Unlike other teenagers, however, the rebellion becomes part of an uncritical stereotype.

People usually do not realize how depersonalizing a stereotype can be until they have been the victim of one. Stereotypes are mistaken for reality. But we fail to recognize that mental images actually create reality to the extent that they become a substitute for getting to know the people themselves. Whatever a PK's motivation for behaving a certain way, the behavior itself can be interpreted to fit a prevailing stereotype. Even mischievous behavior that runs counter to the positive stereotype can be absorbed into whatever people choose to believe:

■ I think that most of the time I was expected to be a very "good" kid. If my friends and I got into trouble, it was assumed that I did not lead us into trouble, but instead got dragged into it myself. I was assumed to be a good kid who got into trouble from his friends—until I was old enough to create my own identity.

Thus ministers' children may feel that, no matter how they behave, whatever they do is not considered on its own merits, but compared with some stereotyped standard. The attitude they meet seems to communicate the unspoken message, "Of course he did that—he's a PK." The result is that some PKs try to hide their behavior from public view because they believe that whatever they do will be stamped and labeled:

■ I tried not to show too much of myself to the general church public, lest they stereotype me. If they didn't know me, they couldn't say I was one thing or the other. I guess I just tried to stay anonymous.

WHY STEREOTYPES MATTER

To an adolescent trying to create a sense of personal identity, rigid stereotypes are suffocating. The drive to synthesize a coherent self-image is so strong that teenagers will latch onto anything that seems to make sense of their existence. Erik Erikson warns that if the only realistically available option is to assume a negative identity, then teens will acquiesce to that, for a negative identity that gives some sense of independence seems more acceptable than having either no identity at all or one that is under someone else's control.[5] Ed Dobson and Ed Hindson recognize the effects of the pressure to be a saint and the potential it yields for rebellion:

Although people would deny it, there is unconscious pressure from most for the pastor's children to perform close to perfection. Others can make mistakes and the mistakes are always forgiven. But when the pastor's children make mistakes, they are sometimes forgiven, but seldom forgotten. Somehow, they are denied the right to be normal. . . . There is a tendency for children to resent this "perfection mentality" and to overreact by doing worse things than anyone else in the church.[6]

Furthermore, Dobson and Hindson observe that the mere existence of a coherent negative image in itself encourages negative behavior:

The converse is also true. Preachers' children think that others expect them to have poor manners, and they subconsciously live up to it.[7]

This is a most appropriate reminder for people who hold negative stereotypes of PKs. In a sense, the image becomes a model to imitate. The testimonies of pastors' children are eloquent on this point. Consider how both positive and negative stereotypes have influenced the following PKs in their struggle for identity:

■ There was, I felt, a tension. My parents expected me to be perfect, and I perceived that people in the church also expected me to toe the line. And yet there was that stigma that PKs have traditionally gone the other direction. There was always that tension between the two. I felt that it was easier for me to opt for fitting in with my peer group; the acceptance was very important. So I went through a period of intense rebellion in which I just completely threw everything out, did the total opposite. I was living the life of the prodigal son for several years. I was still doing well in school, but doing some substance abuse and heavily involved in music and things that my parents were completely opposed to.

■ I went through a rebellious stage, which I basically hid from my parents and the church. They all thought I was the good little Christian I appeared to be, so no one had any suspicions that I may have been doing "worldly things," such as drinking alcohol. Although I was rebellious, I still wanted to live for God, but I rebelled because I was fighting to develop my own identity and attempting to make people see I was human. I guess I also felt I needed God to take notice of me because I felt as though because of Mom and Dad I was unimportant. People get extremely shocked when I tell them I "partied around." Some say I put on an act, but it's because they put me in a mold.

■ I won't detail the pain that I wreaked on my family. Suffice it to say that I became the prototypical PK—untamed, wild, obstinate, hedonistic, a kind of character disorder with a halo. In as many ways as possible, I rejected everything that my father's calling represented: the church, the religious community, and God. I became intimately involved with drugs and alcohol, maintained dead-end friendships, and embraced symbiotic relationships. But as much as I attempted to forge my own identity by systematically rejecting my father's, I concurrently felt deep shame for not living up to my and others' grandiose expectations of what it was to literally be a member of a "family of God." It was the epitomal [*sic*] equation for feelings of profound guilt. And so it was to remain for years, an aggressive attempt on my part to sabotage the façade of "holiness" that insulated our family from what I perceived as reality and my father's passive attempt to maintain the status quo. This culminated in communal feelings of anger, distrust, and inadequacy; and unfortunately, in our case, the maintenance of a conspiracy of silence and denial.

Stereotypes put people into boxes. These images only serve to save us from having to deal with people as individuals. For someone who is trying to develop a sense of identity, rigidly imposed stereotypes are more than just boxes—they may feel like coffins.

So are PKs rebels or saints? Let's not even ask the question, for it assumes that there is a legitimate answer. We must refrain from making sweeping character judgments that are based on small samples of behavior and large doses of expectations. This is especially true once we recognize the effect that stereotypes have on the people who must live under them.

In the final analysis, we are all sinful rebels, yet through redemption God counts us as saints. So who's to say? Are our stereotypes putting stumbling blocks in the paths of pastors' kids? If so, the apostle Paul confronts us: "Who are you to judge someone else's servant? To his own master he stands or falls. And he will stand, for the Lord is able to make him stand" (Rom. 14:4). It is neither our task nor within our power to make pastors' children into saints. And if we do not give up our stereotypes, our "little saints" may become rebels—but not without a cause!

NOTES

1. Alan E. Bayer, Laura Kent, and Jeffrey E. Dutton, "Children of Clergymen: Do They Fit the Stereotype?" *Christian Century* 89 (1972): 708.

2. In William E. Hulme, Milo L. Brekke, and William C. Behrens, *Pastors in Ministry: Guidelines for Seven Critical Issues* (Minneapolis: Augsburg, 1985), 73.

3. Alyene Porter, *Papa Was a Preacher* (New York: Abingdon-Cokesbury, 1944), 17.

4. S. L. Carson, "Presidential Children: Abandonment, Hysteria and Suicide," *Journal of Psychohistory* 11 (1984): 534.

5. See, for example, Erik Erikson, *Identity: Youth and Crisis* (New York: Norton, 1968), 172–76.

6. Ed Dobson and Ed Hindson, "Why Preachers' Kids Go Bad," *Fundamentalist Journal* 2 (May 1983): 12.

7. Ibid.

CHAPTER FIVE

What Did You Expect?

The stereotypes of ministers' children as rebels or saints are, like all stereotypes, too simplistic to have value. As we have seen, imposing these kinds of images can be detrimental and counterproductive. Treating stereotypes as if they represent reality prevents us from knowing people directly. It also blinds us to our own role in shaping their behavior—as when we give PKs a reason to rebel and then make the "observation" that this is, after all, "what PKs do." Fortunately, many pastors' children report that they have not been overly burdened by stereotypes, and some have had the good fortune not to have experienced them at all.

Nevertheless, even if church members cannot truly be said to hold a stereotype of ministers' children in common, they frequently have expectations of some kind: how PKs should act, what they should wear, what kinds of friends they should have, or what careers they should choose. At one end of the spectrum, church members may keep their observations to themselves, making their expectations little more than idle thoughts. At the other end, however, they may actively communicate their expectations as a list of "shoulds," either to the PKs themselves or to their parents.

Of course, all children are surrounded by social expectations. Adults have many different ideas about how they wish children to behave and grow up. Because it is the adults' responsibility to train children and transmit a sense of values, some expectations are necessary. Children will be rewarded in some way for fulfilling the expectations and punished for failing to achieve them. But these expectations, even for non-PKs, are not always realistic. In a major study of American mothers, Louis Genevie and Eva Margolies reported that

> the majority of women of all ages and educational backgrounds (about 70 percent) were neither realistic nor pessimistic, but extraordinarily illusionistic in their visions of what motherhood would be like. Their unrealistic fantasies ran the gamut from slightly romanticized notions to fantasies of perfection: perfect children, perfect mothers, and perfect families.[1]

The question is whether expectations are more for the child's benefit or for the adult's. Parents may fantasize about perfection, but in relatively functional families, parents sooner or later give up their fantasies in favor of reality. They recognize that their child is not an extension of their wishes, but a separate individual with needs. In dysfunctional families, however, the boundaries remain blurred, and the child who disappoints the expectations of parents may be continually harangued for bursting the bubble. Parents who live through their children have tenacious expectations indeed.

The situation is different for PKs—not because they are sometimes expected to be perfect, but because of the variety of sources from which the expectations arise. In forming their identities, young people try to balance the many expectations of people who are important to them: typically, family and peers. For the PK, however, the circle includes church members and the larger community. Other children do not live in close interaction with congregations, do not face simplistic stereotypes, and are not required to be models for peers. You may recall the words of one PK in chapter 4: "It's amazing how many 'parents' we seem to have."

Some church members seem to feel it is both their right and their responsibility to hold PKs to a higher standard of behavior:

> ■ I remember running around the church yard, just being a typical kid, and I was approached—actually, nabbed—by one of the congregation members. He lectured me as to how it was improper for a preacher's kid to behave in such a way. And as he was lecturing me on how I should behave, I was watching his kid do the same thing.

Most families would resent it if someone outside the family presumed to lecture their children on their behavior. They would be doubly incensed if that person did not hold the same standards for his or her own children!

Church members, then, are part of the team of "script-writers" who define the expectations for pastors' children. They may not be fully conscious of this, nor may they realize how strongly these expectations are internalized in the developing PK's sense of self. In a self-reinforcing cycle, some PKs begin to define their identities on the basis of congregational approval. Expectations are repeated through every verbal and nonverbal interaction. Praise and encouragement are extended for self-sacrificial behavior. And even when punishment or rejection are not explicit, PKs may feel that the slightest misstep risks a disaster. Avoiding this perceived threat may require disowning parts of their personalities and denying their real feelings. In this way the identity they have formed in the church context becomes hollow, a mask to be worn in church and removed at home. One minister's son describes how the script was impressed on him and the eventual result of playing the role:

> ■ You grow up within the church, and a lot of people, whether consciously or subconsciously, throw a lot at you—a lot of their expectations: telling you how wonderful you are and how wonderful your family is because you do thus and so, you give so much of yourselves, or your parents were there to help a person through a crisis, or we somehow portray an image that we have it all together. You hear those sorts of things time after time after time, and you fall into the habit of portraying things as all fine.
>
> One of the biggest devastations of my life was when my wife divorced me. It was first of all very difficult because this was the first major catastrophe to happen in our family. What was this going to look like to the church? What was this going to look like to the family of God, who, we knew in our social realm, saw our family as the next closest thing to God? Because every Sunday when they come to church, they see your father up there and your mother leading Bible studies and what-not. It was a difficult time because our image was tainted.
>
> My wife told me one reason that she was divorcing me. She said, "You and your family put on a real act. I know you're hurting at home, but when you come to church, you act as though everything is rosy and fine, just hunky-dory. I'm tired of that lie." That really hit me because that is something that I had dealt with for years and years: How do you live out the life that God has given you, with the responsibility you have to people? Because as soon as I set foot on the church grounds, I am immediately surrounded by people who have needs, hurts, and fears. And what do they do? They come running to the pastor and the pastor's family. I want to be real and find people that I can be real with, but at the same time I want to appear as though I've got it at least somewhat together because of the numbers of people who come my way for support and help and prayer.

A DIFFERENT SET OF EXPECTATIONS

What are the distinctive expectations that set PKs off from their peers?

Students of the Bible. PKs are expected to be avid Bible students and know more about it than their peers.

■ My mother always expected that if there was a quiz or a Bible test, we would win. She just assumed that we would know more than all the other kids.

Sometimes they are conscious of failing to live up to the standard:

■ I was almost embarrassed to a point in Sunday school because there were kids in the classroom who knew more about the Bible and Bible stories than I knew.

Models in Grooming and Appearance. Many PKs are expected to be well-groomed in appearance or dressed in a manner befitting their role. One PK resisted being typecast as the "pretty little pastor's daughter":

■ Once I hit junior high, I was determined to be what I wanted to be and to wear what I wanted to wear. My poor mother used to tell me, "You can't wear pants to church!" She tried as long as she could to keep me wearing a pretty little dress to church. When she couldn't do that anymore, she kind of threw her hands in the air.

Leaders in Worship and Ministry. PKs are often expected to contribute to worship services through music, Scripture reading, preaching, or greeting guests. One girl never knew exactly when she and her sister would be called on to perform musical duties:

■ We were expected to sing on cue. There were many times when whoever was leading the service would say, "So-and-so's going to sing a solo for us," and we just got up and sang a solo. We were expected to be prepared at all times. So we always had one or two songs that we knew, and on the way to the platform my sister and I would usually look at each other and name a song, and that was the song we sang.

Another felt as though the well-being of the church rested on her performance:

■ I felt responsible for the happiness of the church, the attendance, and church growth. I felt that if the church was going to grow, it depended on my faith. I had to be at church all the time and be smiling all the time. It was a very natural thing for me, and I think it was mostly my personality, to greet everyone— not maybe at the door, but at their seats. We moved around a lot, but always to small churches. And it was my responsibility to go and say "Hi!" to everybody. It's funny how I enjoyed that—in some ways, the congregation was my family; they gave me attention. Now I look at it and say, "That was weird."

In a case like this, it is not always easy to point the finger and say whose expectations she was fulfilling. From other stories this PK told me, it is clear that both her parents and the churches they served enjoyed having her play this role, and it seems to have fit with her natural tendencies. Somewhere along the line, however, the role took over and the person was lost; the boundary between the script and life itself became nearly impossible to detect.

MATURE BEYOND THEIR YEARS

Who knows for certain how that minister's daughter may have been trained from birth to take her place on the stage? PKs may have an important role to play in the congregational drama, and the part comes fully, if not always clearly, scripted. Pastors represent their churches, and PKs in turn represent their parents:

> ■ We are supposed to be like our father: His person is supposed to have rubbed off on us. Therefore, immature acts would be seen as contrary to the people we are supposed to be.

To the extent that the pastor is captive to ideal images, so too is the PK unless the parent actively intervenes. The spontaneity and impulsiveness that are normal to childhood are frequently discouraged, and PKs are expected to be miniature adults, with an emotional and spiritual maturity far beyond what is reasonable for their age. Murray Leiffer states:

> The family of no other man in the community is subject to so much scrutiny as is that of the minister. . . . Just as the man himself should be one of the best illustrations for the validity of his own teaching, so he and his family in their mutual relationships should exemplify Christian love, understanding, and forbearance. Parishioners expect to see these attitudes in the wife of the pastor and sometimes, unfairly, look for a poise and maturity in his children which they would never demand of their own.[2]

In chapter 3 we saw that many ministers' children grow up in families and churches where emotions are dealt with realistically and openly. This is part of being allowed to be real children who are still learning about their feelings. Some PKs cannot remember facing expectations beyond those of an average and typical child:

■ I was not expected to act more mature than other kids because we had a great church. They knew and understood that I was a child like any other.

Moreover, while some PKs view themselves as being more mature emotionally than their peers, they do not see this as a negative consequence of enforced expectations. Rather, in the ministry environment they are confronted early with the needs of others and are encouraged to develop qualities such as charity and perceptiveness long before their friends do:

■ We don't need to act emotionally mature: We are more emotionally mature than the average teenagers because we have seen a lot more than they have.

■ It has made me more mature emotionally because I was confronted with people who had problems and I had to know how to communicate and help them. Now it helps me to understand different people and maybe help them.

■ I think it had positive rather than negative effects on me. The positives are that I am perceptive about people and situations, I am not easily swayed from my beliefs, and I can be a support to others.

Other PKs feel that the expectation to be more mature, to set an example for other children, has meant that they could not be children themselves. For the developing identity, this meant they were not able to be themselves, not accepted for who they really were.

Setting an Example

Ministers' children have experienced these expectations in a variety of ways. There are the occasional annoying comments from church members about how PKs should act. One biographer quotes one of Billy Graham's daughters, reminiscing about an incident at a Baptist church. Her brother's naturally childish behavior drew a scornful comment:

Franklin was quite wigglesome and chewing gum loudly and whispering and whatnot. After church a lady sitting behind us said, loud enough for us to hear, that Billy Graham's son should not behave that way in church. We were sort of indignant that she should think we should act any different from other children.[3]

One PK eventually learned to comply with the expectation, at least externally:

■ When I was seven or eight, a Sunday school teacher told me I should stop running around as if I owned the church. I didn't think I was: I was just being a kid. The church was where I played; it was my other house. It made me mad that other kids didn't have to act according to their father's profession. After a while I figured out that people were looking at me. So I tried not to give them anything to look at.

It is important to note again that people are intolerant of childishness in PKs because the children are viewed as representatives of their parents. It is not that childishness itself is wrong; it could be overlooked in someone else's children. But pastors' kids are often aware that the standards for their behavior are not based on rules about children, but on rules about pastors. Another child in the church who runs around or chews gum is just being a kid; but a PK who acts immaturely is a poor reflection on the family:

■ I remember feeling as though I had to act perfectly obedient and knowledgeable, especially in Sunday school or church. This pressure didn't come directly from my parents, but from the feeling that people were watching me and expecting more "ladylike" behavior of me. I felt I always had to act happy, too. If I didn't act happy, then maybe that would be a bad reflection on our family, and I didn't want that. I feel that when I'm out in public, I still put on that act sometimes, as if I have to prove to people that my family is great.

Furthermore, pastors' kids are often quite conscious of being held up as examples for other children to follow:

■ I had to grow up a lot quicker than most. Where others were excused from behavior because "they're still young; they'll grow out of it," I was expected to think harder about my actions and choose to be mature because I was expected to be an example to others.

Setting an example includes how children should dress, as we have already seen in chapter 2:

■ I was brought up to believe that I was to be an example to all the kids my age in the church. When the other kids wore slacks to church, I wore a dress.

These are extensions of the rule of examplarity that *all* members of the clergy family are expected to follow:

■ At the churches I've been at, you're expected to set an example for all kids your age. Therefore you have to be more mature. I think this is so because the preacher is supposed to be an example for the congregation to follow. So is his whole family. This has affected my present life by my feeling I always have to set an example. I can't be myself sometimes.

What is the price of being a role model? Models focus on behavior, and their identities are tied to how well they comply with some external standard of judgment. But where is there a sense of grace in any of this? The external focus can be overdone to the point of sabotaging a secure internal sense of identity, particularly a spiritual identity that rests in the grace of God. One PK is unclear whence the expectations arose, but she clearly recalls the feeling of having to maintain a certain reputation:

■ I'm not sure if this pressure was silently imposed upon me by my parents or the congregation, or if it was my perception of what I was supposed to do. I have always felt that my Christian reputation or "model" was very important to uphold. This continues today, as I try to live up to the high expectations that I set for myself. Sometimes it seems that grace just isn't sufficient, and I must share Christ with the "model" that I present before others.

Another PK remembers trying to keep all the rules and regulations of a conservative denomination. She had internalized the rules well, which meant that she succeeded by external standards of behavior. Inside, however, her spiritual identity was plagued by a lack of peace and the relentless feeling of not measuring up:

■ The basic rules of life, such as why I shouldn't steal, were carefully explained, and though they didn't make a great deal of sense to me, I didn't feel overwhelmed by them. However, I did pick up a load of guilt later on. I believe it was from the combination of my oversensitive conscience and the conservatism of our rule-bound church. I wanted to please everyone—God, my parents, my church, my community. I did pretty well with everyone but God—I could never manage to meet all of his rules, so I kept asking his forgiveness in repeated salvation experiences and kept trying harder.

Many of the church's rules made no sense to me, yet I felt guilty if I broke them. So I became very confused about the difference between true guilt and false guilt, between God's commands and people's rules. Even though inside I harbored a repressed rebellion, on the outside I was a very dutiful child. Even though I have sorted through most of those issues, during times of stress I find myself regressing to the concept of God as judge and me as hopelessly guilty.

Perfect behavior is no guarantee of a well-adjusted identity. Pastors and their spouses already know the burden of having to be perfect for everyone else's sake, with nowhere to turn themselves. Adults may be able to cope with this for a time, but what about children? How do they learn that it is all right to experience emotional turmoil of one kind or another and to feel helped and supported as they try to come to grips with it? The pressure to model perfection seems to exclude this from the PK's childhood.

> ■ People didn't acknowledge I had emotional problems because they felt our family life was perfect. I was expected to lead things, be able to pray better, to have more spiritual gifts, etc. At the moment, I am still expected to be emotionally together and spiritually mature, so people come to me for support. But they don't feel as though they need to support me or that I need support at all.

Growing Up "Old"

Like everyone else, PKs need to be allowed to grow out of childhood into adulthood, and the teenage years in between can be awkward and difficult. To ministers' children, it may seem that childhood and adolescence are both pushed aside by the demand for maturity:

> ■ I think that people, once they learned my dad was a pastor, just assumed that I wouldn't struggle with the issues adolescents go through, almost as if I skipped them. I felt that I was supposed to always act like an adult when I really wanted to act like me, like my friends. It was tough to be myself.

As adults, PKs may become introspective about what happened to childhood:

> ■ I have always told people "I was born older," explaining why I never went through a childish or rebellious phase. I am now forced to consider if my maturity is, in fact, contrived. It may very well be.

Another PK, now a minister herself, reflects:

> ■ As I look back, I feel in many ways that I had no childhood. I grew up old.

In all fairness, we must recognize that these expectations are not always "intentional." Ministers' children often find themselves surrounded by adults, who are present, not to play, but to transact some kind of church business. In such situations, childish behavior is an annoyance:

> ■ As a PK, I was around adults and put in situations with adults a lot more than my un-PK friends were. Consequently, I had to act older or more mature in those situations. I felt that acting my own age was not mature enough. I would get a funny look or comment from a church member and change my behavior and attitude to something more acceptable to adults.

What child hasn't been made to feel "in the way" when adults are about their business? This need not be a problem, provided there is enough time for adults to focus on children as well as their own concerns. But sensitive PKs who are perpetually required to keep their feelings to themselves, so as not to be a nuisance, may soon lose the ability to express the feelings at all:

> ■ My parents were around adults constantly, and because I was with them, I had to be another adult. I am most strongly affected today emotionally—I do not express thoughts and feelings inside me easily. When I communicate, I have to work to attach any sense of charisma to my speech and body language because there were so many times when my thoughts and feelings were secondary that I went ahead and squelched them.

Childhood as Discipleship

True maturity grows out of a long process of "discipleship," in which children and parents are intimately attached to each other. Parents who are emotionally mature themselves can be honest and appropriately vulnerable with their children, nurturing that same kind of vulnerability in turn. Yet as adults, the parents also teach their young disciples how to deal with the emotions expressed until they reach maturity.

An "enforced" maturity is a defense against vulnerability. Consider the perceptiveness of this minister's son:

> ■ There is an extent to which expectations of behavior are either placed upon, or taken up, by the PK. In an environment like the church, emotions in members are continually being dealt with. Emotional instability and extremes of personality or behavior are considered, even unconsciously, as weakness or a sign of a lack of spirituality. Emotional maturity is considered a quality that indicates a strong, proper, and "normal" (if there is such a thing) person. Undoubtedly, emotional "maturity" is displayed by many PKs by forming barriers to feelings or refusing to be vulnerable.

The defensiveness is two-sided. On the one hand, as the quotation suggests, PKs may display the desired "maturity" to protect themselves, to guard against having their real feelings rejected. On the other hand, the decision is like participating in a conspiracy to guard the parents' insecurities as well. Parents who are unconsciously threatened by their children's emotions may tell them to "grow up," to act like adults—in short, to keep their feelings to themselves. One PK reflects on the consequences of his father's rigid "discipline":

■ My father expected us to be perfect children. Spankings and tongue-lashings were very common. So was keeping our hands folded on drives in the car. I am very repressed, not able to express true feelings very well.

This minister's daughter is quite conscious of the unspoken agreement that required her to act more mature than she was:

■ I was always mature and very serious and carried a heavy burden of responsibility for our survival. My dad had major problems in his life, and the rest of the family in effect pledged to protect and cover for him.

Spontaneity of feeling and behavior is supposed to be an intrinsic part of growing up, but pastors' children are often denied that right. One PK, now a middle-aged professional, still harbors much resentment toward the church and a strong ambivalence toward religion altogether:

■ I was emotionally "mature" as I was growing up. Part of the reason was that I was always known, always the preacher's kid. Since I was a compliant child, the expectations from my parents, teachers, and classmates made me behave maturely. I was not interested in causing trouble. My older siblings had done that, and I did not want the conflict they had encountered.

I lost the ability to be spontaneous. I was always controlled and looked mature. I didn't laugh too loudly or cut-up. I was really repressed and often depressed. My behavior as an adult continued in that pattern, with regular bouts of withdrawal and depression that I thought was maturity. When we had children, I began to realize what I had missed as a child, and I began to learn from my children what spontaneity is. I spent a lot of time with my children, partly out of reaction to the abandonment I felt from my family and church, and partly out of the need my inner child had to be free from the maturity I had forced on myself.

Although this PK probably has a long way to go in repairing his personal and spiritual identity, he has begun to meet the grace of God through the gift of his own children. How much better it would have been to have met it through the church!

AND WHAT ARE YOU GOING TO BE WHEN YOU GROW UP?

Related to unreasonable expectations of maturity is another way by which congregations and clergy parents can hinder a child's progress toward self-identity: the expectation that PKs will follow their parents into the ministry.

The careers young people choose should reflect and reinforce the identities they have constructed during their teenage years. They have already spent many hours of childhood play imagining themselves in this role or that—in a sense, trying them on to see how they fit. When a person actually embarks on a career, the choice should ideally serve several related purposes:

- Make use of one's most cherished talents or interests
- Be consistent with the self-image
- Meet the approval of important adults, especially the parents
- Preserve, or at least not seriously challenge, the family's sense of identity
- Have value to the larger community

It may take some trial and error to determine a career that meets as many of these criteria as possible.

Note that only the first two criteria are largely internal, while the latter three are mostly external. What happens if internal and external demands conflict? How many parents have said, "I want you to be a doctor," even when the child wanted to pursue a different career? Some parents try direct coercion: "If you go to medical school, we'll pay for it somehow. But if you go to art school, you're on your own, kid." Parents may believe—not completely without justification—that they know what's right for their children and must therefore lay down the law for their children's sake: "He/she will be happier as a doctor." But people cannot be forced to be happy any more than they can "find themselves" by having someone simply hand them their identity. These parents deceive themselves if they think that their children will suddenly wake up one morning and discover that Mom and Dad were right all along!

Viewing PKs as representing their parents often includes subtle group pressure that they follow their parents' footsteps into the ministry. PKs may feel this pressure very early in life:

■ When I was about age twelve, a woman asked, would I be a pastor like my father? My heart said no, but that would have been a disappointing answer to her. If I said yes, that would have been personally dishonest. So, being very clever, I said, "I will be a pastor, but only if the Lord calls."

It is a clever response, indeed, but how many times can a person use it? If the question is asked too often, the PK may rebel. Ed Dobson and Ed Hindson write:

This is a pressure commonly applied to the pastor's son. Many well-meaning saints ask him, "Are you going to be a preacher like your daddy when you grow up?" After being bombarded with this question for years, the son rebels against it and in many cases rebels against the ministry altogether.[4]

Pastors' daughters also are expected to take up the mantle in some socially sanctioned way. If her denomination ordains women, she may be expected to enter the pastorate. If not, she may be expected to fulfill her calling through missionary work or by marrying a pastor.

Many PKs have entered the ministry and have remained faithful to the criteria we have listed for choosing a career. But a person is not automatically suited for or called to the ministry solely by being born into a pastor's family. Pastors' children who are struggling to maintain an identity separate from their parents' may feel that entering the ministry is tantamount to personal suicide. So it was for Richard Roberts, son of evangelist Oral Roberts, according to Richard's estranged wife Patti. Here is her assessment of why Richard resisted joining his well-known father in the television ministry:

> Richard had been hurt too much. He had been poured into too many molds in his life, and, when I met him, he was struggling to find the courage to break free. I think he resisted joining Oral in the ministry because he recognized, whether consciously or not, that to do so would mean relinquishing his last chance to establish an identity for himself.[5]

Biographer David Harrell notes that there was both a personal and a professional need for Richard to establish an independent identity.[6] Richard had, in effect, protected his boundaries by being a rebellious son, until Patti convinced him to join his father. Now the boundary and identity issues emerged in full force, according to Patti:

> It was becoming more and more apparent now that the only option Richard thought he had anymore was to become Oral, Jr. He would take his father's sermons out of the archives, study them, and then go preach them verbatim. . . . I realize now that this was a critical period in Richard's professional life. He was still insecure and unsure of where he fit in the ministry. Preaching Oral's sermons grew more out of his fears and uncertainties than out of a conscious attempt to recreate himself in Oral's image.[7]

The pendulum swung the other way, from rebellious son to almost a clone. Neither option affords security. The identity struggle continued, through his eventual divorce from Patti, a remarriage shortly thereafter, and the media reaction both events entailed. It seems reasonable to speculate that Richard eventually managed to achieve a more independent identity, but not without great personal cost.

To Choose or Not to Choose

It is necessary to distinguish between expectations and calling, and whether the boundary is clear or muddy depends in large part on the parents and the congregation. Some PKs gratefully recall how parents genuinely respected their career decisions:

> ■ My folks had this beautiful philosophy regarding raising children and their choice of career. Simply put, it was: Encourage, guide, and be available for advice—but never push your children toward a specific vocation. I am sure they prayed a lot about our finding God's will, but they refused to do any more than make very general suggestions. They raised us to be adults, and when we were, they treated us like adults.

A clergy child like this one is not treated as an extension of the parents; he or she is not coerced into ministry, but respected as an individual. If such children decide to enter some form of ministry, it will be *their* decision, not someone else's. They are encouraged to find God's will for themselves, and the parents in turn refuse to play God.

Other parents take a much more direct role in influencing a child's choice of career:

> ■ My father has always wanted us all in the ministry. My parents introduce me to single seminarians and send me brochures from missions organizations. Dad and I had *big* fights about it.

Sometimes the parents direct their children *away from* the ministry, as suggested by the case of another well-known pastor's son: Sir Laurence Olivier. Olivier hailed from a multigenerational heritage of clergymen and was readily expected to follow in the tradition. As a boy, Laurence was immensely impressed with the theatricality of preaching, the way that a talented preacher could manipulate the emotions of an audience:

> My father was an effective preacher, and as a boy, sitting watching him and others in the pulpit, I was fascinated by the way a sermon was delivered. . . . The quick changes in mood and manner absorbed me, and I have never forgotten them.[8]

But, Olivier's biographer notes, his mother did not want another minister in the family.[9] She herself had once vowed never to marry a minister: Unfortunately, Gerard Olivier took the call three years *after* they were married. Watching Laurence stack boxes to form a make-believe pulpit to preach from, she decided to channel his energy away from the ministry and into the theater. She encouraged him to recite monologues from plays instead of making mock sermons. Olivier recalls the profound influence of his mother on his career choice:

She would mouth the words with me, and whenever I stumbled she would urge me on, applauding deliriously when I got it right and suffocating me with hugs at the end. Soon she started inviting other people in to watch me perform. . . . I suppose you could say that I decided at a very early age that acting was for me.[10]

Thus Laurence was to become the first actor in four centuries of the recorded history of the family. It should be noted that to his father's credit—and young Laurence's great surprise—the minister recognized his son's innate talent and eventually encouraged him in the performing arts.

For Olivier, the prospect of being called into the ministry seems to have been eliminated at a fairly early age. Other PKs continue to wrestle with the career issue throughout adolescence and early adulthood, sometimes even after they have already entered the ministry. Those especially who resolve either to avoid the ministry or to leave it must come to terms with two realizations that non-PKs may take for granted: (1) Fulfilling the Lord's calling is not the same as meeting human expectations, and (2) one need not be in a formally recognized ministry to serve God. This sample of statements from PKs illustrates how many have wrestled with feelings of guilt and doubt about their calling:

■ I'm fighting because I've seen the hurts churches cause and what you have to give up and experience. It's hard going into a ministry being aware of how sacrificial it is.

■ I struggled with the idea of becoming a missionary. I even started college with the intention of going overseas. I felt it was my duty and obligation to be in the ministry. It wasn't until I was out from under the cover of being the PK and attending a church on my own at college that I realized God had a calling for my life. I didn't have to do anything simply because it was expected.

■ I've struggled with "should I be a missionary?" but I definitely have come to terms with the fact that I will be what God chooses for my life, regardless. All through high school, though, I struggled with it.

■ People many times assume that I will go into the ministry. But I have never really had the desire to do what my dad has done. I sometimes wonder if my career choice is insignificant and selfish.

■ At times I felt guilty if I didn't pursue the ministry, as if I weren't living for the Lord. In fact, after a year of doing something else, I resigned and became a youth minister for a couple of years. This career change may have stemmed from perceived pressure to serve the Lord through ministry. I have now come to the conclusion that I can serve the Lord in whatever I do, but it has taken hours of prayer-wrestling, thought, and sage advice to feel the freedom to serve the Lord through other means than "ministry." God wants us, not our careers.

A Pilgrim's Progress

Here is a deeper look at how one pastor's son has struggled with career and identity issues over many years. Though he resisted at first, he gave in to the inner urging to enter the ministry. Eventually, however, he decided it was not for him, and he had to deal with the decision to leave the pastorate.

■ I think the biggest issue for me growing up as a PK has been vocation, career choice. As I reflect on it, I chose to be a minister out of a kind of love-hate relationship with the church. In so many ways I hated growing up in a pastor's home. Yet I felt an inner push to follow in my father's footsteps, to remain in that identity of church leadership. It is only now that I am able to process some of these circumstances and feel as if I am entering a field because I feel that I want to do it. That has been a very enjoyable part of my life, the last year or so. But that was such a big struggle for me, trying to work through some of these heavy, power-packed issues, complex issues in making a choice for a career.

When I first went to college, law was where I wanted to go, so I started as a history major. But my mind was constantly hearing these voices, so to speak, that the church was where I should be. Add to this that people who knew me were constantly making comments like, "Oh, you're so gifted," because I'm very musical, and I perform well in front of people, speaking and so forth. And I have a gregarious, warm nature about me. So people were constantly pushing me in this direction, saying, "You need to think about the ministry." So I started to talk about it with Mom and Dad.

I think that once Dad knew I had an interest in ministry, he got excited about it, and then my relationship with him became a little bit more complex. Even though I never felt he was in any way coercing or even heavily encouraging me to go the ministry route, I think it was very satisfying for him that I decided to go in that direction, particularly since he was going through some health problems at the time. He was at a low ebb emotionally with his own self-esteem, and he saw me as carrying the ball.

I think that, aside from my rebellion, this has been one of the most complex issues I have had to deal with. I have enjoyed ministry, yet some of the same issues that I went through as a PK have made life miserable in the ministry, namely, the visibility and people's expectations. That has just been impossible for me to live with.

I came to the point last year of deciding that I am not going to live with this for the rest of my life. I felt that I had to do something about it. It was an extremely traumatic decision to make because of my father's feeling very positive about my being in the ministry. And I was succeeding by the church's standards; they see ministry as specifically formal pastoral ministry. So I had to work through some very complex issues.

When I made the decision, I felt like Bunyan's pilgrim—a whole load had been lifted from me psychologically. I felt much more inner peace, though it was very difficult dealing with the church and telling them I wanted to go in a different direction. And telling my parents I wanted to go in a different direction was difficult, too. But I did come to the point where I said, "Look, I've got to do what's going to really make me function on a good level as a person, with the inner peace I need." Those are some of the reasons I have done what I have, and I feel very positive about it. But several generations of my family have been with this denomination, and it has been complicated to make that break.

Reading the Script Correctly

It is possible for children to misread and misunderstand the "script" written for them. Internalized expectations can be illusive, especially when clear and open communication is not the rule. Children who are left to their own devices to decipher what others expect may distort or exaggerate expectations in the process. If there is little communication, they will not have the opportunity to verify what they perceive.

This is the case with one PK who was descended from a long line of pastors. His father, a successful minister in a large church, was a forceful man, tending to sweep the children along with him in the way he interacted with them. The son felt obliged to follow the family tradition and so entered seminary. He wrestled, however, with the feeling that the pastorate was not for him. He came to realize that he actually wanted to pursue graduate studies in another field, yet he felt certain that his home church and his father would not approve, seeing him more or less as his father's successor.

Nevertheless, he made the journey home and told his family and congregation that he had other aspirations than the ministry. To his amazement, they supported him completely and even confirmed the direction he had chosen as a good fit with his talents and gifts. Needless to say, that minister's son is now studying in a field that is much more to his liking and that he feels is his particular calling from God.

The script that defines the role of the PK can be very complicated. There are potentially as many subtle variations as there are people in the congregation, perhaps more. Children orient

---

Do You Expect PKs . . .

To act more maturely than other youth their age?

- By expecting their conduct to be an example to other youth in the church?

- By expecting them to act more like little adults than like children?

To follow automatically in their parents' footsteps?

To know more about the Bible than other youth in the church?

To be more closely involved in the church ministry than other members?

To be well-groomed in appearance, especially ministers' daughters?

To "have it all together"?

---

themselves by adult expectations; but when the expectations are too numerous, too rigid, too all-consuming, children are left in a quandary. Do they live up to the expectations and lose something of themselves in the process? Or do they rebel, find their own way, and risk the rejection of their extended family? One minister's daughter said, "How can the kids realize that they don't have to live up to everybody else's expectations, that they can be normal children?" And one might add, how can they realize this and still maintain a sense that they are God's children?

Pastors' kids must be treated like any other member of the congregation, with the same guidance and the same support. Above all, they must be respected as individuals in their own right and not be expected to function as ideal role models or surrogate pastors. In this way they will have the latitude they need to come into a sense of personal and spiritual identity that is truly their own.

They are, after all, normal people like everyone else. So what did you expect?

NOTES

1. Louis Genevie and Eva Margolies, *The Motherhood Report* (New York: Macmillan, 1987), 5. This study was based on a survey, conducted in 1985, of 1,100 mothers in the United States between ages eighteen and eighty.

2. Murray Leiffer, *The Layman Looks at the Minister* (New York: Abingdon, 1947), 129.

3. John Pollock, *Billy Graham: Evangelist to the World* (San Francisco: Harper & Row, 1979), 141.

4. Ed Dobson and Ed Hindson, "Why Preachers' Kids Go Bad," *Fundamentalist Journal* 2 (May 1983): 12.

5. Patti Roberts and Sherry Andrews, *Ashes to Gold* (Waco, Tex.: Word, 1983), 55.

6. David Edwin Harrell, *Oral Roberts: An American Life* (Bloomington: Indiana University Press, 1985).

7. Roberts and Andrews, *Ashes to Gold*, 86–87.

8. Quoted by Anthony Holden, *Laurence Olivier: A Biography* (New York: Atheneum, 1988), 15. The original source of the quotation is a BBC-TV interview with Kenneth Tynan in 1967.

9. See Holden, *Laurence Olivier: A Biography*, 12ff.

10. Quoted by Holden, *Laurence Olivier: A Biography*, 16. The source of the quotation is Thomas Kiernan, *Sir Larry* (New York: Times Books, 1981).

PART 3

The Players

CHAPTER SIX

PKs Are Not All Created Equal

In the drama of identity, part 1 of this book examined the "stage" for pastors' children, that is, some common characteristics of the social environments in which PKs are raised. Part 2 looked at the "script," the role definitions that emerge from oversimplified stereotypes and the expectations of congregations and clergy parents. The danger is that in rewriting the script we may regroup all ministers' children into a new, improved stereotype!

As we have seen, not all pastors' children play out their lives on similar stages. The boundary issues and communication rules vary from situation to situation. If there are scripts to be acted out, they are not all the same. One point of this book is to tease out the factors we should consider in looking at the life of any particular PK. Each environment provides a unique combination of concerns.

Every drama must have a stage and a script. In large part, however, the success or failure of the play depends on the performers who are cast for the various roles. Some roles, it seems, could be performed by nearly any competent actor or actress. Others are more difficult, and casting the wrong person in a role can have unfortunate consequences for even the best of scripts. Moreover, the cast must all be able to work together, to meld their performances in a "chemistry" that makes audiences take notice.

Part 3 will take a look at the "players" who make up the cast in the PKs' drama of identity. Each cast member makes a different contribution to the drama as a whole. Subsequent chapters will examine, in turn, the roles of parents, peers, and parishioners. In this chapter we will consider how pastors' children develop as individuals. The characteristics they are born with define both the range of roles that fit them and the scripts that will be urged on them by eager "casting directors."

DIFFERENT FAMILIES UNDER ONE ROOF

I have often heard parents (and sometimes their adult children) say something like "I don't know how the kids came out so differently. They all grew up in the same family, and we tried as best we could to treat them all the same way." The implication is that children are all born as blank slates, waiting for the parents to inscribe their futures and their personalities. There are at least two mistaken assumptions here: (1) The family environment has not changed over time, and (2) how the parents treat their children virtually determines how the children turn out.

The first assumption does not take into account that the addition of each child changes the family and makes it different. A family with no children is different from a family with one child, and both are different from a family with two. Look at this from the children's point of view. The oldest child may remember a time when there were no younger sisters or brothers requiring the parents' time and attention. The younger siblings have never known a time without older siblings. All the children share a common name and live under the same roof, but the "family" that the older children can remember is not the same as the one the younger siblings know.

The second assumption fails to recognize that even if it were possible for parents to be perfectly consistent from one child to the next, their treatment of their children is not all-determining. We are compelled to resort to the old "nature-nurture" controversy: How much of a child's personality stems from innate factors, and how much from social factors? On the one hand, few question the importance of parental behavior in a child's life. On the other hand, isn't it evident that many children are different from each other right from the start? The first child may be sleeping through the night within the first few weeks and is never picky about food. The second child, however, is still having problems with sleep at four years old, and he or she doesn't like to eat anything but peanut butter! What did parent behavior have to do with forging those distinctive characteristics? The startling similarities reported between identical twins reared in separate homes seem to indicate that parenting may play a much smaller role than we generally imagine.[1]

Most observers of human development take a broad view, contending that this is not an either-or question, but rather, nature and nurture interact. Gender offers a good example. The biological sex of children is a given. Their eventual *gender identity*, however, is the result of a complex give-and-take between biological and social factors.

Parents may try to be evenhanded with sons and daughters in many ways, but may still communicate differences in expectations. Ironically, these differences in treatment may be circularly justified by sex-linked stereotypes. One family disciplines sons more strictly than daughters. The parents believe that boys have a wilder spirit that must be tamed, while girls "need" less domestication. Another family is more lenient with sons than with daughters because boys must be allowed to "sow their wild oats," while girls must be trained in proper behavior. And both families believe that their child-rearing practices accord with the "nature" of girls and boys!

Needless to say, when it comes to building a sense of what it means to be male or female, nurture adds a great deal to nature.

Pastors' children, of course, are children first and PKs second. As individuals they are as different from one another as other children are. These individual differences influence how each PK experiences being reared in a pastor's home. Not all children in a particular clergy family turn out the same way, as the following observations from minister's children attest. First, a son:

■ I probably had a harder time being a PK than my brother, since he was a supportive and helpful person and was happy to fulfill the responsibilities placed on him. I, however, being rebellious, would buck and complain and whine. I have found that in most families of two there is a more placid, accepting child and a rebellious, more difficult sibling.

A daughter:

■ My brother has always seemed strong in the Lord and never had the desire to rebel or express or claim independence. My sister and I fought against church stereotypes. We mildly rebelled and fought against decisions Dad made, but our brother was always on Dad's side. My sister and I conformed to some expectations of the church against our true will in order to keep Dad and the church happy. But my sister had particularly bad hurts, so she rebelled more and expressed her true feelings more.

One could speculate endlessly about why the experiences of siblings in the same family and church environment are so different. In the first example, the son hints that the brothers were different "by nature"—one helpful, the other rebellious. Do any innate character traits account for this? In the second example, did it make any difference that the ones who rebelled were the daughters, while the son took the father's side?

To distinguish some of the ways in which they differ from one another, I asked PKs to compare themselves with their siblings. Who had a harder or easier time as a PK? What do they think accounted for the difference? My purpose in asking PKs about sibling differences was to factor out, if possible, some of the environmental considerations. My observations are sorted into three categories: differences in gender, sibling position, and talent and temperament. In real life, of course, the three are not separate. A PK's gender, where one fits in the birth order, and the inborn character traits all blend with various social expectations to create the unique experience of each child in the family.

We must keep in mind that much of what follows is a kind of second-order speculation: I have asked PKs to speculate on sibling differences and have in turn speculated about their speculations! I hope, however, that these musings will be sufficient to illustrate what makes one PK different from another and emphasize the importance of treating PKs as individuals in their own right.

GENDER: OF DAUGHTERS AND SONS

The first consideration is the child's gender. Daughters and sons, whether inside or outside the church, are often held to different standards. Brought to bear in the clergy family, these social norms can create differences in the PK experience even for siblings in the same family and church environment. One minister's daughter, for example, is fully convinced that daughters feel more pressure and expectations than the sons. Her reasons arise from her experience: Her behavior and physical appearance were watched more closely by the congregation than her brother's were.

■ My brother wasn't as concerned with his looks. He looked fine, but he wasn't saying, "Oh, no! Bad hair day!" And he wasn't obsessed with his weight.

Now, clothes and hairstyle influence status and acceptance for boys as much as for girls. But for boys this is largely a matter between peers, not so much what adults think of them. And it does seem to be true, at least in the American culture, that the range of attractiveness in appearance is narrower for girls. It is more common for girls than for boys to be greatly preoccupied with their appearance, even to the extent of developing eating disorders such as bulimia and anorexia nervosa. Eating disorders are not uncommon among the ministers' daughters in my survey. It is not clear, however, to what extent this can be attributed to cultural values of beauty or to churchly expectations.

A Double Standard

Some comments from PKs suggest that in some cases there is a persistent double standard in how parents and congregations treat them. Both parents and congregations may be more "paternalistic" toward girls. One minister's son recalls that his sister faced more expectations than he did. He observed, for example, that his parents allowed him to date at a younger age than her. A daughter's social life may attract more public concern than a son's:

> ■ I don't think people were quite as concerned about whom my brother was going to marry, or when he was going to marry, or whom he was dating.

The double standard can be carried to great extremes. Behavior that would be considered improper or unacceptable in the minister's daughter may be tolerated in the son simply "because he's a boy." One daughter related that her father was restrictive and protective about her dating and that both parents would not even acknowledge the possibility that she might experiment with drugs or sexual activity. But for her brothers, the situation was different:

> ■ My father knows that my brothers did cocaine and marijuana and had sex with girls—but they're boys, and that's fine.

If one were to ask the pastor, would he say that all these behaviors were "fine" with him? Probably not. Nevertheless, his attitude toward his sons' behavior appeared to be different from that toward his daughter's. This contributed to her sense of being treated unfairly and added to the pressure of being a preacher's kid.

Yet the double standard can work both ways. Sons may experience some pressures more than their sisters do. The feminist movements have opened many doors through which women have gained acceptance in what were once considered "male" roles in a male-dominant society. The perception of men, however, has not advanced much. It is still more socially acceptable for a girl to be a "tomboy" or a "daddy's girl" than it is for her brother to be a "sissy" or a "mama's boy." One minister's son wrote:

> ■ I am the only boy in a family of sisters. At times I feel it is harder being a guy, as there are pressures to "not be a sissy."

A minister's daughter believes her brother had it harder being a PK, "because boys are supposed to be tougher and find it hard to believe in such a power as the Lord." Peers may regard religious devotion as weakness, or they may recast the "little saint" and "goody-two-shoes" image as "sissy" behavior. For pastors' sons trying to form a personal and spiritual identity, this is an unnecessary added weight.

The Place of Feelings

We have discussed the importance of one's being free to recognize and communicate feelings. Chapter 3 dealt with the implicit rules that originate in the internal needs of the system, rules designed to prevent the disillusionment and instability that would result from honest communication. This condition may be complicated by the tendency in our society to train males in ways that incipiently hinder males from dealing openly with emotions. One minister's daughter felt that her brother had a more difficult time being a PK because, "being male, it was less acceptable for him to express his feelings, and this made him introspective and quiet." Are pastors' sons thus placed at a social disadvantage early on when it comes to learning to speak the truth in love?

In any case, it appears that some differences in PK experiences can be traced to gender differences. The net of expectations they are born into will depend to some extent on the "accident" of nature that made them male or female. A first step, then, in recognizing the individuality of pastors' children might be to ask ourselves whether we are harboring any different expectations for daughters as for sons.

SIBLING POSITION: THE BLESSINGS OF THE FIRSTBORN?

Gender is only one environmental factor that accounts for differences among PKs. Birth order—where a child fits in the line from oldest to youngest—is another. Gender and birth order together comprise what Walter Toman calls "sibling position."[2] Toman contends that (1) the experiences of individuals who share the same birth-order position in a particular arrangement of brothers and sisters will be similar, and (2) these experiences are transferred to relationships outside the family. For example, Toman's research suggests that oldest brothers in families with all boys will develop similar characteristics. These traits will be different from the youngest brothers, who in turn bear a resemblance to one another.

In some families and cultures, sibling position defines the

"pecking order" of both privilege and responsibility. This was certainly true in ancient times, as shown in the Old Testament tradition of the *birthright*—the privileges of inheritance and blessing that came with being the firstborn son. When Rebekah was still heavy with Isaac's twins, the Lord made what must have been a startling prediction: The older of the two boys in her womb would serve the younger (Gen. 25:23). Sure enough, this younger twin, Jacob, coerced his famished brother, Esau, into trading his birthright for a bowl of stew (vv. 29–34). Note, however, that Scripture does not chide Jacob for his scheming; rather, Esau is denounced for his cavalier attitude toward the privilege that was rightly his (v. 34; Heb. 12:16–17).

Later on, Jacob tricked his father into giving him his older brother's blessing (Gen. 27), which left Isaac shocked and Esau incensed. Even years afterward, Jacob feared that his brother might still hold a grudge (Gen. 32:7–8). And ironically, near the end of his life Jacob intentionally reversed the blessings on two of his grandsons, giving the firstborn blessing to Joseph's younger son instead of the older, to Joseph's displeasure (Gen. 48:17–20).

In contrast to this value system, however, many firstborn PKs do not view their sibling position as a privilege. There are common disadvantages to being the oldest, among them the tendency of parents, in effect, to "practice" on their first child and gain from the new experience. The oldest child may see this as unfair, since the younger siblings seem to get better treatment. A pastor's daughter writes:

■ I think Mom and Dad learned with me and were able to improve in their handling of my younger brother. We made it, though—I learned to forgive.

Another comments, "Since I was the firstborn, I became the experimental model, so in a way, I had a harder time than my brother and sister."

The eldest is the first to go through all the important developmental milestones that may trigger parental anxiety. Issues such as rules of discipline, school performance, public behavior, dating, and curfew are hammered out between the parents and the oldest child first, and this may make the way smoother for the younger siblings.

■ I think perhaps that I had the hardest time being a PK, if only because I was the first one; I had to break the ground for the other two.

■ I think my older brother and I had the hardest time as PKs. It's always we older children whom people seem to look at, but perhaps my other siblings will have their hard times soon, too.

■ The older sister always meets higher expectations, and I was the younger sister. I guess she forged the way.

■ Being the oldest, I felt that I had it harder because I was always the first to do anything, such as go to school, etc. So people always found out that I was a PK, and when my siblings came along, they just accepted that they were too.

■ I'm a middle child with older sisters. Basically, I was able to get away with a lot and watch what they did and avoid certain circumstances that I saw them go through. In a way, I had it easier.

■ My younger sister was never an angel, but she never really rebelled either. I think I went ahead of her and opened a lot of the difficult doors, and she just followed in my wake.

One anticipates that both clergy and congregations will modify their unrealistic expectations somewhat after their experience with the eldest PK. If so, this may pave the way for greater acceptance and tolerance with the younger ones. Yet this may offer small consolation to the firstborn.

Acting Like Adults

A common theme among firstborns is the pressure they feel to occupy more responsible, adultlike roles in the family than their younger siblings. In this regard, Kevin Leman lists what he calls "axioms" of the firstborn, among them these four:

"Everyone depends on me."
"I can't get away with anything."
"I was never allowed to be a child."
"I never said I wanted to be a role model."[3]

These axioms seem to apply poignantly to eldest PKs. In chapter 5 we observed that PKs generally are expected to be more mature than other children and are held up as role models. Firstborn ministers' children in particular live with a dual expectation: to be examples not only to their peers in the congregation, but to their siblings in the clergy family. The eldest may have to bear adult responsibilities such as involuntary baby-sitting for the overworked and absent parents. Firstborn females may even become surrogate mothers:

■ I used to be very proud of the fact that I was the oldest. Now I really see how that has affected me, in my taking care of the whole family. My mother did not take that role often; she was too tired,

I guess, in her role. I was like a second mother to all the children and was often asked to baby-sit. They never had to go through that. I don't think they even took care of each other, and they would gang up on me. It just wasn't age appropriate.

Another firstborn surrogate mom speaks of the emotional outcome of having to bear much responsibility:

■ My parents referred to me as their "built-in baby-sitter." I felt responsible for my siblings' well-being, often protecting them from my parents' rages and disappointments. I grew into an adult with an overly tuned sense of responsibility and still have difficulty with guilt over what is not accomplished in any given day.

Firstborn PKs may identify unduly with their parents' occupational stresses, taking on their frustrations at an inappropriately early age:

■ My oldest sister tended to become more bitter and protective of Mom and Dad. The rest of us were a little less obvious. Because she was slightly older when we went through any rough times, she got more involved and understood more of what was going on.

The firstborn may keep their behavior in line, not just because they believe this is right, but so as not to burden their parents:

■ I'm the oldest, and I think I felt responsible to set a good example. My parents didn't deserve the grief of rebellious kids.

And some take an even more responsible role, trying to protect the entire family from its difficulties:

■ I think for me—this is typical of a firstborn in any family—that the firstborn is the one who tries to keep the family unit together, who tries to cover the family or shield the family if there are any problems. Many times I was just exhausted, as I've looked back at my life and the tremendous burden that I've carried on my shoulders—of trying to present to the church a family that had it all together.

The problem with bearing this kind of responsibility is that it tends to push the PK's own needs aside.[4] Children should have their needs cared for by adults, not the other way around. This is how they grow in confidence and security and eventually become able to be responsible to others. But some firstborn PKs may be handed a large burden of responsibility before this foundation is properly laid. Their identities become overdependent on taking care of others. Later in life they wonder where their childhood years went. Never having had their own needs adequately addressed, they feel a sense of hollowness in the core of their self-image.[5]

Sometimes the legitimate childhood needs are well acknowledged by the congregation or the clergy family. In these cases, the image of the responsible PK can offer a viable identity to the child who has the talent and temperament to achieve it. Many firstborn PKs do in fact achieve it, with zest. Yet this leaves a tough act for younger siblings to follow. We saw in chapter 1 that younger PKs often find themselves in the shadow of successful older siblings who are active in the church. The younger ones are expected to measure up to the standards of achievement set by older brothers or older sisters. As we shall see in the next section, this is a problem when the younger siblings simply are not as talented in the ways that their families or congregations value. An eldest pastor's daughter reflects on the identity challenges faced by her sister:

> ■ My younger sister is having a hard time with the expectations that generally come with being a PK. She's not *really* rebellious, but she's tried to get away from being a PK. She's said that she wishes she wasn't one. I think having an older sister close in age makes it hard, too. She wants to be her own person, just as I did—not the pastor's kid or my younger sister, but herself.

Respecting the individuality of pastors' kids must include recognizing that younger PKs should not automatically be expected to walk in the shoes of successful older siblings.

The Timing of Transitions

There is a corollary to sibling position in the *timing of family transitions*. Several PKs suggest that factors such as when the family entered the ministry or when they moved from one church and school district to another, taken together with their age at each transition, constitute a crucial part of their experience. One PK observed, "I think each child struggled less straight down the line. It may have to do with the ages at which we became PKs." Children who are older at crucial transitions may have more freedom from any hardships entailed:

> ■ I think I had it easier because I was older than my brothers and sisters when Dad went into the ministry; I was already in my mid-teens. I had more freedom to go and do my own thing, to escape from the house when I needed time alone.

An eldest daughter was also a teenager when her father entered the ministry. To her mind, this gave her an important advantage over her brother:

■ My brother had a harder time just because he experienced the lifestyle longer than I did. He is *still* in rebellion and hasn't had anything to do with church since he left home.

This eldest had already flown the nest when the trouble started between his family and the congregation:

■ I had it easier because by the time Dad was getting frustrated with church leadership, I had left home. It scared my sisters, and they have only recently come back to the Lord. They carried the burden for Mom and Dad even though they could not help them.

In short, the sibling position into which PKs are born is a significant part of their experience. Being a firstborn may entail becoming the "guinea pig" or facing greater expectations of maturity and exemplarity. Depending on when the parents entered the ministry, it may also mean having a better chance to escape some of the restrictive expectations that the younger siblings have to endure. Having a later position may spare a PK the pitfalls that elder siblings have already negotiated—or it may mean having still another model to live up to. Whatever the arrangement in a particular PK's family, sibling position is one more dimension to understanding ministers' children as unique individuals.

TALENT AND TEMPERAMENT: I CAN'T HELP IT; I WAS BORN THIS WAY

The concept of an inborn *temperament* figures strongly in the nature-nurture debate.[6] The notion is that children are born with certain biologically based characteristics that vary in degree from child to child. For example, some children are more regular in their biological "rhythm": they eat, sleep, and perform bowel functions in a regular and predictable manner. These children are much easier to train than their less predictable siblings and generate less frustration for their parents. Another example is a sensitivity to stimuli. On one extreme, the parents of one boy I know used to let him take his daytime naps right on the carpet; his mother could vacuum around him, and he would sleep through the noise. On the other extreme, parents have related that they very gingerly put their child to sleep and tiptoe out of the room, only to have the child wake up screaming when they turn on a light at the other end of the house!

Other innate characteristics include how well and quickly children adjust to new situations and people, whether their general mood is positive or negative, and how active they are. Certain combinations of temperamental qualities make a child easy to live with and easy to love; other combinations make parenthood much more trying. Everyone adores the child who is adaptable and easy-going; it is hard to like a child who seems to be perpetually cranky and hypersensitive.

Reading the Labels

It is crucial to recognize that these traits are given to the child at birth, for a great deal depends on how parents react and what labels they use. It is one thing to recognize that some children adapt slowly to new situations and need time to adjust. Parents can teach these children how to deal with their tendencies constructively and plan an "adjustment period" whenever the family faces a new transition. It is another thing, however, to say instead that these children are "shy" or even "antisocial." Over time, these labels create their own reality, leaving the children with a sense of helplessness to change themselves.

The matter of what labels parents place on their children is an illustration of what Stella Chess and Alexander Thomas call "goodness of fit."[7] Simply put, the traits children are born with may or may not match their parents' expectations and abilities. Where there is a poor fit, parents are very likely to blame the children by labeling them as inadequate, rather than recognizing that the problem cuts two ways. For our purposes we can identify the problem as an example of poor boundaries, inasmuch as the parents may be unable to take the children's behavior at face value and can only see it as a disappointment of their expectations.

Chess and Thomas offer a fascinating illustration in the case of "Nancy" and her family. Nancy was a temperamentally difficult child, slow to adapt, and given to displays of negative emotion. Her father held rigidly to his expectation that she be more easy-going. Because she was unable to comply, he became critical, labeling her a "rotten kid" and complaining about her freely to others outside the family. Fortunately, in the fourth and fifth grades Nancy demonstrated considerable talent in both music and drama—arts that her father valued highly. Although her temperament had not changed, her father's perception of her had: She was no longer just a "rotten kid," but rather an "artistic personality." With that new label in mind, he was able to relax his expectations and allow room for her to grow in her own way.[8]

How does labeling apply to PKs? Every pastor's child is born with a particular cluster of temperamental traits, talents, and potentials. As a pastor's child, he or she is heir to numerous expectations.

For one child, the combination of what is expected and what is possible will be a good fit. The more easygoing PK who is also talented musically and academically may find the saintly PK role a natural fit. One minister's daughter was a compliant and well-behaved child who sang well and enjoyed church life. Her identity is firmly grounded in the church and in her relationship with her mother:

■ I was the good kid, and I always did what was expected of me. When I was quite young, I made a commitment of my life to the Lord, and I felt the call to be a minister's wife. I always had the desire to do that. I would say that I have very much modeled my life after my mother. I had a lot of respect for her, and our temperaments are very much the same. I really respected her and wanted to be like her. I think that had a lot to do with being called.

Another child may be more naturally inclined to negative moods and a fierce expressiveness. Pastors' children themselves paint a broad portrait of the characteristics that seem to make for a poor fit in congregational life. Stubbornness and the tendency to fight back figure prominently:

■ I think I probably had a more difficult time than my little brother and sister. I'm extremely independent, aggressive, and goal-oriented. I'm also less patient than most people. I know what I want and whom I want to be. I don't want anyone else to get in my way or tell me whom to be.

■ My sister wants to go back into the ministry, to "follow in their footsteps." I guess she must think it was great—or at least bearable. She never rebelled. So perhaps it was easier for her than my brothers and me. She is fairly high-strung and emotional. I am very laid back and sensitive—but I don't get "hurt" and whimper; I strike back. She never had confrontations with church members as I did—and they always compared us!

■ I think that because I'm the oldest, more stubborn, and more "emotional" than my sister, I had a little more trouble with being a PK than she did.

■ I was more questioning and rebellious toward the church than my sister, so I clashed on more issues. She accepts without question—I never did.

■ I think I found it harder because of my temperament—stubborn, rebellious, and holding grudges.

■ My temperament was—*is*—much different from that of my brothers. I'm much more independent and strong-willed. I needed to know "why" for everything and needed to be known and liked for *me*, not as the preacher's kid or the little sister. My brothers did not have that need as strongly and were more content in general. I am the only one who really went through a period of outright rebellion.

■ Compared with my brother, I'm a complete opposite in temperament and commitment to the church. Father places less discipline on his life because my brother is more volatile.

■ My brother had a harder time because he was more susceptible to doing wrong things. He was also more stubborn, which made him stand his ground.

■ My brother is a lot like me in temperament. My sister will probably find it a lot harder. She will probably have heaps of trouble because she doesn't really know how to handle situations well—she's too stubborn and sensitive.

How many of the traits described are actually inborn, and how many are learned as a defense against expectations? And how accurate are the labels? "Stubbornness" seems more like a character evaluation than an objective description. Some ambiguity is inherent in the discussion. It is clear, however, that the PKs themselves accept many of the traits as "natural," and they may be correct. Whatever the case, congregational expectations may well make a poor fit and identity conflicts virtually inevitable.

Conflict Internal and External

The conflict, however, may not be where anyone can see it. PKs who express themselves openly may have repeated clashes with parents or church members. These are very likely to be labeled "rebels"—which, as we have seen, can become a self-fulfilling prophecy. If it can be said that living in a glass house induces rebellion, then it is also true that outward rebellion encourages further scrutiny:

■ My older sister was *much* more rebellious as a teenager than any of the rest of us. She struggled the most as a PK, and I think she was more in a "fishbowl" than the rest because of her rebellion.

Others may appear to be "saints" on the outside, compliant and cooperative, but simmering with unexpressed resentment on the inside. Thus, the rebellion can be internal:

■ I've never talked with either my brother or my sister about their feelings of growing up as a PK. I would say, though, that none had a more difficult time than another. We are all relatively close in age, so we experienced the same stereotypes within the churches. My sister proved to be the most rebellious of the children. Her rebellion would be considered mild compared with the typical idea of rebellion. I, on the other hand, had no *outward* rebellion, though I experienced a significant amount of quiet rebellion.

We see that two PKs in the same family may be rebellious, but one rebels outwardly and the other inwardly. The identity conflicts, however, are no less serious for those who keep their rebellion to themselves. An outwardly compliant minister's son who grew up with more expressive and rebellious siblings described his internal struggle for personal and spiritual identity:

> ■ I perceive my sister as an extroverted, compulsively busy person who has had outer conflict with the church. She has not experienced the grief and inner conflict in the church that I have. My brother is also more of an extrovert than I and has had struggles with the church. As a child he was outwardly rebellious.
>
> I surfaced as a compliant, peace-loving child who wanted to avoid conflict at all costs. I accepted the role of a "good PK" and made everyone happy. I was often compared with my father because I looked and talked like him. This all seemed to go well until I was in my late twenties and thirties, when I began to recognize a lot of ambivalence and anger at the church and Christian school. It took my "midlife crisis" for me to put it together the way I am describing it to you. As a child I sacrificed my true self (feelings and desires) for peace in my family, the Christian school, and the church. Now I am feeling the anger I had toward these institutions.
>
> Unfortunately, connected with all these institutions is the important concept of the relationship to a God. This has been a most distressing area, in which I am working with the fear of abandonment by God and the church in trying to build my own spirituality, one that I can trust.

The Right Stuff

Talents point up another way in which PKs are not born equal. Some are good at the activities and skills valued by clergy families and church members; others are not. Ministers' children who prefer activities outside the church may receive little support and therefore find it more difficult to incorporate these activities smoothly into self-identity.

> ■ I had a harder time being a PK than my sister. She seemed to enjoy it. I hated it. I think the reason is that she enjoyed designing activities and doing things with the church. By contrast, I enjoyed playing sports at school and doing things with friends outside the church. My parents didn't support me in this because they didn't have time. They would spend all their time with the church. Since my sister had all her activities with the church, she didn't mind.

My brother is more like me. He enjoys activities at school. He also enjoys activities at church, so it isn't as hard for him as for me.

A similar story is told from the other side, by a minister's daughter who had the talents that the congregation valued. She sees the unfortunate circle that was drawn in her brother's life between not having the "right" talents and being labeled negatively:

■ My brother, the middle child, had the hardest time with being a PK. School was not easy for him. Behavior problems resulting from this were quickly scrutinized, especially since he followed in my footsteps as well (I was a good student). I excelled in music—which was recognized and used often in church—so I often received acceptance and recognition from my congregation. My brother, however, excelled in sports—and was rarely seen by the congregation. He received less support and recognition. He was quickly labeled a troublemaker.

In such families, not surprisingly, comparisons are drawn between the children:

■ I think I had an easier time than my older sister because I was more secure, confident, and actually more intellectually gifted; and comparisons were made, unfortunately.

This kind of "encouragement" does nothing to help the less-talented or differently talented PK to gain a useful sense of identity. But there is irony in this: The more troubled PK may take up so much of the parents' energy and attention that the sibling who succeeds in the role feels neglected.

■ I feel that my younger brother had a much more difficult time being a PK than I did. I seemed to be able to live close to the model expected of me, and I also did very well in academics and athletics. My brother seemed to have difficulty living up to the image imposed upon us and to my accomplishments as a big brother. My parents did everything they could (so it seemed) to make our lives equitable. They bent over backward at times to make living easier for my brother. In fact, it seemed that the more rebellious he got, the more attention he received. I felt gypped.

Although the more talented sibling may be considered more fortunate in some ways, he or she still needs to be properly and regularly encouraged and not taken for granted. The challenge is to do this in such a way that other siblings do not feel devalued by comparison.

PUTTING IT ALL TOGETHER

We have seen that gender, sibling position, talents, and temperament mark important differences among the children of ministers. For some, one of these dimensions may play a more crucial role than the others in the PK experience. For others, the interactions weave a more complex tapestry. Note the interplay of gender, birth order, and apparent temperamental differences in this story from a minister's daughter:

■ I have two older brothers. Of the three of us, the eldest brother definitely had the roughest time. The structure of the church and the restrictions placed on us were a little too tight for him. He reveled in breaking rules and causing distress. My other brother is more easygoing and takes things as they come. He wasn't exactly a model teen, but he fit the criterion better and worked with it. I don't feel I had a tough time as a PK. As the only girl, it was harder for me simply because my parents seemed to be more protective since I was also the baby of the family.

Another example of the complex interplay of identity factors comes from a minister's daughter who has sisters but no brothers. So there are no gender differences, but the temperaments seem to vary, expressed in how the girls responded to their father. The oldest experienced the most difficulty and demonstrated the greatest rebellion, in that the father apparently relaxed his standards gradually with each successive child.

■ My older sister did not like being a PK. I remember her complaining about having to be a good example to everyone. However, I believe it was her relationship with my father, rather than his being a pastor, that bothered her the most. During her teen years she became very rebellious and did much to defame my father. The battlegrounds between her and my father were many, but I believe the real issue was my father's domineering personality and his attempts to use force to get her to do what he wanted.

As for me, there was no rebellion against being a PK. In fact, I was proud to be the pastor's daughter. I really liked the recognition it brought me and was proud of my father. His position and strength gave me more of a feeling of importance than was appropriate.

Although I didn't rebel against my father for being a pastor and didn't act out rebellion against him as a person in any spectacular ways, I went through times of intense anger toward him. I can remember feeling very angry with him for being mean to my older sister, who was a teenager at the time. I remember being very angry at him during my own teen years, but also having enough love for him and appreciation of his love to refrain from going to any extremes in disobeying him. Because of what I had seen of his interaction with my older sister, I decided to just avoid letting him in on my life when I was a teenager. I especially tried to avoid letting him know if I liked any boy. When I was college age and my parents were being reasonable with me, there were still times when I was very angry at my dad for the way he treated my little sister and for the way he sometimes treated my mother.

I think the main reasons our responses were different from each other's were our inborn temperaments and the fact that my father was less forceful with me than with my older sister and less domineering with my younger sister than with me. My older sister has a strong personality and had the most to rebel against. My younger sister had less fear of my father than I did, which allowed her to be somewhat rebellious, and she had less to rebel against than my older sister had. She did not rebel to nearly the extreme that my older sister did.

BLOOMING WHERE YOU'RE PLANTED

We must remember that our observations are speculative. Although gender and sibling position are incontrovertible factors, it is extremely difficult to sort out what represents actual inborn characteristics from the labels they might have been given over the years. It is not crucial, however, that we determine a PK's temperament with complete accuracy, even if this were possible. What is important is that we recognize the implications of the concept of "goodness of fit" as it applies to ministers' children.

When a child is born into a family and a congregation, it is like planting a flower in a particular plot of soil. Not all plants thrive under the same conditions: Some prefer sandy soil, a little water, and lots of sunshine; others like denser soil, more water, and shade. If the flower wilts, do we place the blame on the flower, on the physical environment, or on how the flower was tended? All provide only partial answers.

We should not be looking to blame, but to understand. Pastors' children are not specially ordered from the factory to meet either family or congregational specifications; they are born with a unique set of God-given qualities. Some will thrive in a given congregation or family; others will not. When a PK fails to blossom and grow, we need to look at all the possible causes. Instead of fixing blame on the child by labeling with stereotypes, we can try to understand the "soil conditions" and see what we might be able to change.

Above all, we can strive to understand PKs as individuals and, in so doing, respect their boundaries. Of course, we cannot know ministers' children as deeply as God does, for he knows them to the very core of their being (Ps. 139:13–16). But we can seek to love them for the persons God created them to be. This does not mean that we condone their errors and disregard their faults; we all have sinful tendencies and need guidance toward authentic righteousness. But how much of our "guidance" stems more from our misperceptions and self-reinforcing, stereotyped labels than from an honest appreciation of pastors' children as individuals? If we are to teach, guide, or transmit values, we must appreciate and safeguard children's individuality and foster secure identities as persons and children of God. To the extent that we try to understand who they are, we help them to discover themselves.

NOTES

1. See, for example, the cases cited by Peter Neubauer and Alexander Neubauer in *Nature's Thumbprint* (Reading, Mass.: Addison-Wesley, 1990).

2. Walter Toman, *Family Constellation*, 3d ed. (New York: Springer, 1976).

3. Kevin Leman, *Growing Up Firstborn* (New York: Delacorte, 1989), 30.

4. See, for example, Carmen Renee Berry, *When Helping You Is Hurting Me: Escaping the Messiah Trap* (San Francisco: Harper & Row, 1988), especially chapter 2.

5. A related phenomenon is described by Alice Miller in *The Drama of the Gifted Child*, trans. Hildegaard Hannum and Hunter Hannum (New York: Basic Books, 1981).

6. The reader is referred especially to the New York Longitudinal Study headed by psychiatrists Stella Chess and Alexander Thomas. See Chess and Thomas, *Temperament in Clinical Practice* (New York: Guilford, 1986), and their more popular work, *Know Your Child* (New York: Basic Books, 1987). The argumentation in this section relies strongly on their work.

7. See, for example, Chess and Thomas, *Know Your Child*, chapter 4.

8. Ibid., 65–66.

CHAPTER SEVEN

Clergy Parents and Their Boundaries

As we must recognize the individuality of pastors' children, so must we acknowledge that their parents are also unique. Despite any expectations we may have, it is not fair to assume that clergy are either better or worse parents by virtue of their profession. Developing parenting skills is always on-the-job training. Even though a person may need a graduate degree to become an ordained minister, no education whatever is required to become a parent—and parenting skills are not usually part of the ordination exam.

On the one hand, some clergy are marvelous parents. As we shall see, Billy and Ruth Graham were both involved and loving parents. Their five children speak affectionately of their guidance and spirituality. On the other hand, many Christians appear to be much better prepared to play a ministerial role than to raise children. In some cases, PKs protest that they are treated more like members of the congregation than like offspring, in that their parents seem compelled to preface nearly every act of discipline with a long sermon. The Bible may be used as a tool to control children's behavior:

> ■ My father would occasionally take us into his room when we were being bad and would make us read passages from the Bible, ones that usually applied to lying or fighting or cleanliness or temper. . . . That really bothered me and gave me some negative feelings toward Bible reading. If all the Bible did was condemn, then I wasn't interested.

Some clergy parents are even abusive. The case of the late recording artist Marvin Gaye is a well-known example. The driving theme that dominates the singer's biography is his tumultuous and enmeshed relationship with his preacher-father, Marvin Gay, Sr.* The elder Gay, as a child in Kentucky, had witnessed the bloody beatings to which his father had subjected his mother. He, in turn, became a violent, alcoholic father who demanded that his children undress before he beat them. Marvin, Jr., rather than meekly submitting, would purposely provoke the beatings. His friend and biographer, David Ritz, interprets his life as a never-ending search for his father's unattainable blessing. The relationship between the two Marvins was forever one of mutual antagonism, culminating in the day that the father shot his son to death.[1]

Is this an isolated case? I know a PK who was ritually beaten by her parents, often to the point of bloodshed. I have communicated with others who have been molested or sexually abused in other ways by their fathers; some of the abusive pastor-fathers, like Marvin Gay, Sr., were alcoholic.

> ■ My dad preached from the pulpit about love and respect and then came home and hurt us. My mother wanted perfect children who were no trouble. My dad was also an alcoholic. People saw him as the most wonderful minister there ever was. At home, he was drunk, sometimes maudlin, often abusive. Mother did not protect us.

Sadly, the secretiveness that characterizes abusive families was compounded in this family by the need to maintain the public image of saintliness. Let us hold no rosy illusions about clergy as perfect parents. Like other adults, they range over the whole spectrum of parenting skills, from wise and loving to unstable and abusive. The issues we have already discussed are part of that spectrum: from boundary violations to healthful communication of feelings; from inappropriate expectations to the ability to recognize individuality.

The focus of this chapter is once again the boundary issues in the clergy family—how parents either help or hinder their children's developing identities by the way boundaries are handled. The comments from PKs in this chapter are arranged to make clear what distinguishes "successful" from "unsuccessful" parenting practices in the glass house, at least from the children's point of view.

---

*The family surname was Gay, but Marvin, Jr., adopted the spelling "Gaye" professionally.

THE IMPORTANCE OF FEELING IMPORTANT

An issue that emerged from my survey was whether or not PKs felt important to their parents. With the demands of ministry relentlessly pressing in, many pastors' children felt neglected. Others, who felt that their parents took time for them in spite of these pressures, were for that reason all the more grateful for their parents' attention. I therefore asked PKs directly: "Did you feel that you were as important to your parents as the ministry? In what ways did they make you feel either important or unimportant?" There are highly instructive differences in the comments between those who felt important and those who did not.

What did clergy parents do to make their children feel important to them? Several related themes emerge from the PKs' comments, but spanning all of them is the matter of the quantity and quality of time spent with the family. In chapter 2 we noted that many congregations seem to consume an inordinate amount of the parents' time and energy. Some parents, however, have made a strong commitment to preserving time with their families amid their other responsibilities. The commitment is more than lip service; it is lived out consistently in taking time for family recreation, to talk, to just be together.

■ If Dad had been busy all week, he made sure to spend some time with us Friday or Saturday.

■ Vacation times were special and sacred.

■ Our family went on two or three vacations each summer. We would go skiing during the winter. Breakfast and dinner were with my family almost always—mostly dinner.

■ I feel I was important. My parents spent a lot of time with us, playing games, going fishing, going on holidays. I basically had a very good life as a PK.

■ They both spent time with their family such as talking and going places with us. My father was a very busy man, but he always made me feel wanted and often found time with us. In the summer we went on trips together.

■ Although Dad's schedule was extremely busy, he always took time for us—a day off a week, if at all possible, for family times. Also, no matter what the schedule, we always met for dinner as a family—this continued through our teen years.

The Children's Agenda

Clergy parents who are committed to spending time with the family demonstrate in a tangible way that their kids are important to them. Equally important is *how* the time is spent. From the children's perspective, it would not be a "family" commitment if the whole time were taken up by talking church business. Rather, if the children are to feel important, the time needs to focus on whatever is important to *them*. This may mean participating in some of their activities and interests, both inside and outside the church:

■ When we were young, our parents encouraged us to be active in the youth groups and took part in them also.

■ I always felt important and special and never "second" in line because of responsibilities or meetings. Dad could rearrange his schedule to come to school to hear concerts or pick me up when I was sick. He actively participated in our scouting programs and extracurricular activities.

■ My parents attended all my athletic activities from elementary school through high school. They attended other school activities too.

■ I felt that I was as important as the ministry to my parents because they always were interested in my activities. I played basketball for four years in high school. They were there to watch me for a majority of my home games and about half of the away games, depending on the distance. They also were at all my band concerts in high school. These are just a few things they did to make me feel important.

Knowing What Is Going On

Family time may mean just taking the time to communicate meaningfully on a personal level. These parents sought their children's input and were genuinely concerned to hear what was going on in their lives:

■ They took time out to see how I was doing.

■ Daddy always had time to talk. I *knew* I was important.

■ I always felt loved, supported, and cherished. I always was listened to, and my problems got careful attention. The church took too much of my parents' time, but that is a rather generic complaint in most professional families. I wouldn't want to do it over any other way.

■ They asked my brother and me for our opinions on family issues.

■ They ask me my opinions and include me in their discussions.

■ Most times, at the drop of a hat, Dad would help me and took time to listen.

■ My father especially and my mother made me feel important to them. I always felt that when I went through a tough time, my parents were there to give moral support.

■ Mom and Dad *really listened* to what was going on in our lives— and they made us feel that our lives, our thoughts, and our opinions were important. That kept us together as a family, built our self-esteem, and gave direction to our lives.

■ My parents were fairly easygoing and always tried to explain things to us. They showed me a lot of understanding, kindness, and love.

Partners, Not Competitors

Taking time with the children, however, does not always mean competing with the church. Sometimes clergy parents find ways to involve the children in their professional lives, by taking them along, finding small tasks for them to do, or appropriately using their talents in the ministry itself:

■ Dad would often ask us for sermon ideas or revisions and anecdotes.

■ My dad would occasionally take me with him when he was away preaching at other places.

■ Every Sunday morning and some weekends we would go to church with Dad to do photocopying and run errands for him.

■ My father would take me to people's houses that had kids my age to help the children open up, too. It was a lot of fun being with my dad.

■ I would often go with my father when he had errands to run or people to talk to.

■ Dad would have me sing with him, which makes me feel important.

■ God has given me a gift in music, and it is used in Dad's ministry in our own church and others.

Not Enough Room for the Children

If these are some of the characteristics of clergy parents who succeeded with their children, it stands to reason that the opposite would be true where PKs were left to feel unimportant. Rather than being concretely committed to sharing time with the family, these parents are too preoccupied with ministry to have room for the kids:

■ A lot of the time I felt unimportant and still do at times as I'm out of the home now. The church socials, meetings, and anytime-of-the-day-or-night counseling put a damper on the time I wanted to go fishing or whatever with my dad. I got tired of being pushed around by the scheduled events of the church. For a while I never wanted to come home because either I'd be alone or there would be no dinner again because of the church doings.

■ All of their time, energy, and money was going to the ministry.

■ My parents would say that we were important, but I did not feel this was the case. After all, all their time and energy went into building the people of the church, etc., etc., etc.

■ I felt unimportant because ministry got preference over me a lot of the time.

■ Our schedule always revolved around the church and other ministerial duties. Vacations were postponed and canceled.

■ At times I didn't feel as important as the ministry. The main reason is the time commitment. Most "ministry" occurs in the evenings and on weekends when the family has the most available time to be together. All ministry is supposedly of God and seems more important than family commitments (the family will "understand").

■ Our lives were shaped around the needs of the church. Having no money because the church needed it, moving to different towns, not being allowed to do things and go places. . . . Dad spent a lot of time on the church and didn't have a lot of time for the family.

■ It's very difficult for me to remember my father ever playing with me in any fashion. When he wasn't eating or sleeping, he was working on the "Lord's work." My mother also spent much time in preparation for Sunday school, Vacation Bible School, youth groups, etc.

Ignoring the Children's Agenda

Instead of participating in the children's interests, the parents show little or no support shown for their extracurricular activities:

■ I did not feel I was as important as the ministry. I played a lot of sports at school; I also was in the orchestra. They never had time to come to see me play because they were so involved in the church. Due to this, I came to resent the church.

■ School functions were missed or not attended with my parents, all because church came first.

■ Family life had to be sacrificed for the sake of the ministry. I was never visited at any of my school days. The best thing Dad did for me was that one day he picked me up when my bike had a flat tire.

Lack of Communication

Another problem in families where boundaries are not defined is a lack of personal, child-centered communication. Pastors' children who feel unimportant remember parents' not taking the time to listen to them or consider their opinions:

■ They are always always always always always always not listening to me because they don't have enough time.

■ Sometimes the going was rough, and they were always talking church.

■ We were never conferred with on any moves; we were just uprooted and carried along.

■ I often felt that decisions were made that didn't take our needs into consideration.

Feeling Used

When parents do involve their children in the ministry, it may be in ways that make the PKs feel used instead of important:

■ It made me really angry when my dad put church before his family. Sometimes if we saw him on Sunday morning, he'd be too busy to say "Hi!" or be nice. He might grab me to help set up chairs or stuff bulletins or hand out fliers. I hated being used like that: "forced service." Once he was setting up tables at church, and I must have asked him the same question twenty times, and he still didn't acknowledge me. Later, he explained that he was setting up and that was more important and I needed to understand that. Well, I saw his point, and ten years later I still remember.

I always wondered how old I would have to be until he would respect me enough not to make me get hot and sweaty setting up chairs in a dress. I'm still waiting to grow out of that.

The end result of this kind of treatment may be a child who feels that no one cares about him and who in turn ceases to care about the family or church:

■ My parents made me feel relatively unimportant compared with the church, and although this hurt for a while, I now do not care about either.

Upstaged, But Not Forgotten

Of course, it would not ultimately be fair simply to divide clergy parents into the two categories of "successful" and "unsuccessful" according to their children's perceptions. The reality of the demands of ministry may mean that even parents with the best of intentions will not be completely consistent. The following PKs express a kind of ambivalence, feeling important to their parents in some ways and at particular times, but feeling upstaged by the ministry at other times:

■ At times I have felt both ways. My parents understood many of the problems of a pastor's family and tried to make sure they were never "winning the world but losing their kids." They would spend quality time, but sometimes the ministry would come first, and we'd feel hurt.

■ They often put the church ahead, but you know that they love you, and you have to accept that. It does get frustrating, though.

■ Yes and no: At times it seemed as if they did not have time for me, but most of the time they made me feel that I was more important than anything else, through spending quality time with me.

■ My parents have a unique ministry. There are activities six days out of the week in the evenings. Christmas is also very stressful. There were times when I would not see my father for days during the Christmas season. It was during these times when I felt that church activities were too important. However, my parents were always encouraging, and they made it clear that they loved me.

■ During one struggle, after which we left that church at the board's request, I did feel kind of "second in line" to the church—though some of that may have been my own fault. But I did feel somewhat abandoned, especially by my father. However, after that, I *never* felt as if I took a back seat to anything. My parents became very involved in my high school activities and were very supportive. My father at times got someone else to lead a Wednesday evening service so he could come to a school concert, etc.

■ Most of the time I felt as if I were as important as the ministry. Occasionally the ministry took precedence over me. I recall numerous times on family vacations we would have to go home due to a funeral. I was always disappointed in the fact that no other minister would be able to perform the service, and we would have to come back. Shortened family vacations, though, are about the only times I can recall in which I felt slighted by my father's occupation.

■ At the time, growing up, I didn't think too much about it. I now believe that my father placed more importance on the ministry. However, while he may not have shown it by spending time with us, I know that he had great love for his children and family. He had difficulty showing it.

■ The ministry was more important, but I'm not sure it was my parents' choice—the organization told them where they would work, in what job, where they would live, what car they would drive, etc. From there I think it was just survival. One move that we made was hard for me because I lost so many friends; at that time my parents made an effort to spend time with me. For the most part, the ministry was first!

WHERE'S DAD?

In discussing ways by which clergy parents make their children feel either important or unimportant, we must qualify our terms. We must take into account individual distinctions and the rich variety of relationships that might be found in a single family. In the first place, not all children in a family will feel the same way; each child's temperament affects how one fits into the family. Second, parents do not always treat each child equally, as when they have favorites or overidentify themselves with particular children.

A third distinction is that mothers are commonly much more involved with the children than fathers are, and this is particularly true in clergy families. Responses from PKs on this matter range from a kind of wistfulness about not having Dad around, to outright resentment of what seems to be self-serving behavior on his part. These PKs had fathers who were either physically or emotionally absent from the family:

■ I think that generally the ministry was more important to Dad, but the kids were more important to Mom. Mom spent time with us—which I think is the biggest indicator of importance. This must be balanced, though, with the understanding that Dad had a twenty-four-hour job to do.

■ My mom was always around and had time. However, my dad spent a lot of time at the church, and to this day I'm not as close to him as I am to Mom.

■ For a long time I thought the ministry was more important than we kids and family life were. But God has called Dad to what he is doing, and we are not missing out; we are cared for. However, I'd like to see my dad more often.

■ My father was a workaholic. I didn't really get to see him. And as for the interaction between me and my dad, I guess there wasn't a whole lot as I was growing up.

■ The church is really everything in my father's life, and he often said—and still says—"God, church, family," and he does not see that it should be any other way. My father gave to every person in the church—everyone. Everyone in the church got his ear, anytime. But it hurt me over and over again to see my father caring for little kids, my friends, listening to their needs, and not mine—giving my friends hugs, and I wouldn't get hugs.

■ We were and are important, more so to my mother than my father. My father is more worried about appearances and façades rather than his marriage's health and real survival and his children's emotional well-being.

■ Mother certainly was balanced, but father was committed to nothing but *himself*, not even ministry—he used it to gain for himself.

■ So many needs of the family were overlooked because there were just constant demands from the family of God. Being in a pastor's family, or being a PK, means your dad doesn't have weekends off; with other kids, their dads are always home on the weekends. In your friends' homes, their dads are home at night; in our family, Dad was gone. He was counseling, leading Bible studies, leading board meetings. There was always something going on in the evening, and there were very few evenings when he was home. It was the family or the church, and most of the time, the church won out. As I look back on my life at some of the things I've had to work through, one of the biggest is that my dad was gone so much.

Absence and Boundary Violations

Is being routinely absent from the family a problem in itself? Is it accurate to say that the less time a pastor-father spends with his family, the less "successful" he will be with his children?

An extensive body of research seems to link father absence with numerous difficulties in a child's life.[2] But some researchers have challenged these studies as simplistic. It is too easy to say that the pragmatic solution is for pastors to spend more time with their families. That may be a good start toward a solution, but at least one research team has concluded that merely getting Dad more involved is not in itself necessarily better for the children![3]

How, then, should we understand and apply what these ministers' children have told us? I believe it is helpful to see a father's absence and its larger context as a boundary problem.[4]

First, the inordinate demands of the pastoral profession on one's time and energy fit Boundary Violation 1: "Congregations expecting too much of the clergy family's time and energy."

Second, we must recognize that congregations are not wholly to blame. Many pastors implicitly support this arrangement, however loudly they may complain. Despite the large amount of time and work required, pastors derive much satisfaction and self-gratification from

How Clergy Parents Can Make PKs Feel . . .	
Important	**Unimportant**
They are firmly committed to having family time together.	They are too preoccupied with church matters to have time for their families.
They take the time to listen to their children's feelings and opinions.	They are too busy to listen to their children.
They support and participate in as many of their children's activities as possible.	They show little or no support for their children's extra-church activities.
They involve their children in the ministry in appropriate ways.	They use their children in the ministry in intrusive ways.

their profession. This is not wrong in itself. The problem comes when the pastor is either unwilling or unable to set boundaries between church and the home: Boundary Violation 2.

In many clergy homes, the combination of these two boundary violations makes it almost impossible for the pastor to break free either physically or psychologically from church obligations.

Protecting the Family

Some ministers' children express appreciation for their parents' continual efforts to keep a clear boundary between church and family, making family life as "normal" as possible:

■ They involve us as much as they can, but they try not to let church life interfere too much with home life.

■ I always knew that I was important to my parents. They protected us quite a bit from the criticism and the "fishbowl" situations. They tried to make our home as normal as a layman's home—no difference! (Usually!)

■ They treated us like normal kids and led a normal life. The ministry was just a job.

According to one biographer, the kind of protectiveness that these PKs express was characteristic of Billy Graham's family. John

Pollock makes these observations while quoting two of Graham's children:

> Apart from strict orders to refuse interviews, the children were protected from fame so well that they were unaware of it. . . . The children spent a normal childhood, out of the limelight. "The home atmosphere," Ned recalls, "was not really affected by my father's position as an evangelist as far as I could tell." It was a normal home, with parents "who never let me down." . . . The children were never featured as public examples of a Christian family but had a healthy sense that home, in Franklin's words, "is private and personal; it is not for the world to see."[5]

QUALITY OR QUANTITY?

I discern two truths in our discussion of what makes PKs feel important or unimportant in their families: (1) the difference lies not in the quantity of family time, but in its quality, and (2) this qualitative difference is a matter of boundaries. Naturally, as it is often said, we cannot have "quality" time without some "quantity." Parents should not deceive themselves into thinking that a few minutes a week with the children is sufficient even when those minutes are packed with meaningful relationship.

There is probably some minimum amount of time—determined by temperament, age, and other factors—that each child needs from each parent to establish a sense of importance. Beyond this threshold, a clergy family will not necessarily be more "successful" regardless of the time spent together. Quantity itself is not the issue. The crucial factor is the demonstrated commitment to spend time and what this commitment represents: the ability to set clear boundaries between church and family. A well-marked boundary gives children the security of knowing that they have ready and reliable access to their parents, so they will not feel abandoned when the church calls.

Clergy parents can be physically home for much of a day, but emotionally absent. This is because even when they are home, they may be preoccupied with church matters and let the stress of the ministry spill over into family life:

> ■ I think that in some ways it was a little difficult relating to Dad. Although we had time when we could laugh and just have fun with him, when he did come home, it was usually time to get out the belt, so to speak. This complicated our relationship. He was seen as the "big heavy"—he had to be the one to give us the discipline. And I think that because of the complex issues and the stress he was feeling in his job, he would more often than not discipline out of anger, frustration, and impatience.

I see discipline as more related to some of the issues that my parents were going through and their inability to deal with some of the stresses of life, and not so much an integral part of raising us as kids.

■ The way I first noticed problems with the church was in my parents' relationship. They did not deal with the stress effectively. They started arguing a lot. Then I would hear references to such-and-such a person. My parents kept these stresses from us as little kids; I guess they didn't want to burden us. But there was no way around it: As a child, I knew what was going on. Their silence was more deadly than their speaking about it. And then, when they started talking, they'd talk too much to me about it.

Sometimes the spillover seems to be almost intentional:

■ We had to be good because Dad had enough to deal with at church. Dad raged at us, and Mother said he had to get mad with us because he didn't dare get mad at the congregation members who were making him angry.

In this instance, the parents' inability to keep an emotional boundary between work and home results in further violating the children's boundaries.

Boundaries Between Generations

One particular type of boundary violation is something that family therapists call "parentification."[6] In relatively healthy families, there is a boundary between the generations: Adults and children have different roles and responsibilities. It is the parents' responsibility to look after the well-being of their children. Sometimes, however, roles are reversed, and children find themselves elevated inappropriately to the status of an adult—in effect, having to "parent" their parents.

This parentification is not problematic if it happens only occasionally; it can help children learn empathy and care. But when it occurs repeatedly and often, the children's personal boundaries are violated. Sometimes the parentification is subtle, as when PKs feel they must keep their problems to themselves to avoid upsetting their parents' emotional apple cart. But when the parentification is too great, PKs become emotional surrogates for their parents, standing in for emotionally absent adults. It is not coincidental that all three of these PKs were the eldest children in their families:

■ I kind of held the family together. I was the placater, the rescuer. I was the one who functioned like the parent. My parents weren't the parent. I was like the surrogate father for the whole family. That was a tremendous pressure.

■ I was placed in the position of being my father's surrogate spouse, assistant-pastor kind of person, going out and doing ministry with him. My dad would also confide in me. Now I understand the bad feelings that I was having when I would talk to my father about that. It was an incestuous type of thing with my dad when he was confiding in me. He went through a lot of pain for months, but wasn't really able to share it with anybody except me. He would talk with me about it. Now I wish I had been able to say, "Forget it, Dad. Don't cry on my shoulder."

■ Because Dad wasn't around a lot, and I was the oldest, Mom would use me as an emotional crutch. She would talk to me about her problems. I'm not sure how healthy that was for a little kid. She would complain about Dad and would release some of her pent-up emotions about his not being there for her. It kind of put me in a bind because sometimes Mom and Dad would have interchanges, and I would say something bad about Dad or go on Mom's side, and Mom would say, "You can't say that."

When I got into junior high, basically what I did was turn the TV on, and that was my escape. I became a TV addict. All I would do is watch TV, and emotionally I would shut everybody out. That's how I dealt with the problem.

Note the children's responses in the second and third cases. The second PK, in retrospect, wishes that she had drawn a boundary by telling her father not to bring her his problems. The third PK actually drew an artificial boundary by escaping into the world of television and shutting out his family. These are defensive responses, meant to protect personal boundaries from the intrusiveness of parentification.

Busy, But Accessible

Again, the "quality" issue is that PKs need to know that they have emotional access to their parents. When the parents are preoccupied with church matters, access is blocked. It is doubly difficult to bring needs to their parents when the parents' needs dictate that the children must play more mature roles. Keeping a clear boundary between church and home life helps guarantee the access that PKs need.

This can happen even when the quantity of time available seems less than desirable. Pastors who are frequently gone from the home can nevertheless demonstrate their accessibility and their commitment to honoring family agreements. A story from Jerry Falwell's autobiography shows his willingness to put the family first despite some personal cost:

One Monday morning I was going over my schedule for the week and realized that a secretary had booked me to give the keynote address at a large convention on Jerry Jr.'s birthday. It was a mistake. No one had noticed it until it was too late to get out of the speaking engagement easily. Immediately I called my son to tell him the problem.

"We've made a mistake, son," I confessed. "But we have a family commitment never to miss sharing a birthday celebration. Here are your alternatives. I will give you the $1,000 honorarium that I would receive for the convention address and spend the next day with you, or I will cancel the booking and spend your birthday as we had planned."

One thousand dollars would be quite a birthday gift, I reasoned, especially to a young boy who was already saving for college. But without a moment's hesitation Jerry Jr. said, "I'd rather have our day together, Dad. Cancel your speech."

I cancelled it without a further word. It was embarrassing. It caused those convention officials a great deal of grief and confusion. I apologized to everyone, but spent the day with my son. No matter what dream consumes us, our relationship to God and to our family must come first.[7]

The busiest of ministers can still be accessible. John Pollock shows that this was true in Billy Graham's family:

The children always had an open door to their parents. "It did not matter who they were with," says Franklin, "or where they were. If I wanted to talk, they always were ready to stop and listen." No rule was ever imposed that the children should not interrupt their father at his desk, but they hardly ever did; they feel a little resentful when heedless strangers impose on his time for the mere pleasure of it.[8]

Note that the children respected Billy Graham's boundaries even though no rule was outwardly imposed. Could this be because they knew they could have his ear whenever they needed it? The following story from Graham's middle daughter, "Bunny," makes this point. He was on a tight schedule, between engagements, and she interrupted him with a personal problem:

Busy as he was, he spent time, he loved me, he prayed with me, he cried with me. That will always be a very special memory, that Daddy would take time from his busy and tiring schedule to share his daughter's burden.[9]

A pastor's son offers yet another example. He regretted his father's frequent absences and decided against entering the ministry because of the workload. Nevertheless, he cherished his father's clearly demonstrated availability:

■ My father told each one of the family members that anytime we had a problem, or we had a need, or for whatever reason we needed to talk to him, his office door or his phone was always open to us. It didn't matter that he was in a board meeting; it didn't matter if he was counseling someone who was close to suicide, whatever—he told his secretary, "If any one of my family calls, I will take the call," or "I will see them at any time," or "If I'm dealing with a crucial matter, and they appear at the office, I'll get to them just as soon as I can stop what I'm doing and break away." And you know, my dad did that for me on a number of occasions. I remember coming home during my years in high school in the middle of a traumatic event. The only one I knew who could solve the problem was my dad. I marched myself right on over to the church and knocked on his door. My dad very quickly excused himself, came out, put his arm around me, and said, "What's going on?" *He totally shut out the rest of his world and focused on me.* And, boy, I tell you, my dad, you just can't get much higher—the esteem, the love I have for him because he was willing to do that. I knew I was important to my dad, and I knew that he loved me because he would drop anything to be with me [italics added].

This busy pastor was able to create an emotional oasis for his children, right in the middle of his hectic schedule. When he drew that boundary around his relationship with his son, the boy knew that nothing would be allowed to snatch his father away.

Family Time

Maintaining clear boundaries between church and home means not allowing the demands of the job to intrude on the parent-child relationship. Family time is for attending to the family, not to the church:

■ Our parents always made sure that we realized how much they loved us. I knew this because of the family times we had. When we spent time together, church concerns weren't brought up.

Pragmatically this may mean making firm agreements with family, church members, and staff about when the family can or cannot be disturbed.

■ I felt that we were more important than the ministry. One way they showed us was family night. Every Monday night we would spend a couple of hours together and do an activity (watch a movie, play games, read books). My dad made it clear to the other leaders of the church that this time was ours and asked them not to call if it wasn't an emergency.

Family priorities must be clearly communicated to the staff. Establishing boundaries may sometimes require going away with the children, as on isolated family vacations, or occasionally taking them where people and telephones will not interrupt, as to a restaurant in a different community. The point is that the ministers' children both need and desire reliable and consistent access to their parents. When the children need their parents' attention, they have it:

> ■ I remember that, at church, if I had to ask my dad something, I'd go stand by him and he would never turn me away, even if he was talking to someone—he would acknowledge me.

In this way PKs feel recognized as people and affirmed by their parents. They feel *important*. This is the very foundation of a stable sense of identity.

Lest there be any misunderstanding, let me emphasize that keeping a clear boundary between church and family relationships does not mean keeping the children out of the ministry! As we saw earlier, involving the children in appropriate ways can make them feel important in having a part in a significant element of their parents' lives. The key word here is *appropriate*. The children should not be forced to participate in ways that violate their sense of personal boundaries, as if their lives were only extensions of the parents' lives. PKs should be involved in the ministry in ways that respect their individual talents and preferences.

This is what makes the parents' participation and support in extracurricular activities so important. Children are shaping their identities by the activities they choose. From the very earliest years, children bring their achievements to their parents for approval: a drawing, tying a shoelace, putting their clothes on by themselves— inside out and backwards, perhaps, but still on their own! Later, in school, there are many other activities from which to choose, but they still need their parents' support. The wise parent distinguishes between the activity itself and the function the activity fulfills in helping to create a sense of identity. In so doing, parents can encourage and build up their children's right to be individuals, even when they do not fully approve of an activity. The parents' participation gives the message, "Yes, we are interested in you. We don't just want you to be a part of our lives; we want to be a part of yours."

This grateful PK reflects on how his parents respected his boundaries:

> ■ They were incredibly dedicated to supporting me in everything I did even if they didn't want me doing it. I think they realized I had to learn on my own. They were happy with me for who I was. They were also happy at my accomplishments in sports, journalism, school, work, etc. They were very encouraging. Our lives revolved around God, but family life was important.

BOUNDARIES AND CHRISTIAN IDENTITY

An important corollary to the church-family boundary is the one between pastoral and parental roles. We saw in chapter 1 that PKs can have trouble drawing a clear distinction between their heavenly Father and their earthly fathers. Note how this PK's father, being forceful and dominating, colored her relationship with God:

> ■ I believe my biggest problems associated with being a PK have more to do with my father's strong demeanor, domineering personality, and bad temper than with my having lived in a "glass house." It is also possible that being a PK caused me to be more inclined than most people to view God as being like my father. I believe my father's personality traits have a lot to do with why he chose to become a pastor, and in that sense, my being a PK impacted my life. I suspect that many pastors have personality traits similar to those of my father.
>
> As an adult I have had huge problems with doubting my salvation or worrying that the Lord requires me to go to unreasonable extremes in sacrificing for him. This has greatly hindered my relationship with the Lord and my ability to serve him. I believe in him but have very little confidence in his acceptance of me. Though I have a loyalty to him, I have little love for him.

The close connection between how PKs relate to their fathers and how they relate to God makes it extremely important for pastors to maintain good boundaries. Three elements need to be clearly distinguished: the pastor's identity, role, and responsibilities (1) *as a Christian*, (2) *as a father to his children*, and (3) *as a church professional*. The implications of the boundary between church and family life pertain specifically to the last two elements. The pastor's identity as father and minister should be stable enough to allow him to separate the responsibilities of each role emotionally and pragmatically. His identity as a Christian, however, should permeate and undergird both.

If parents want their children to develop strong spiritual identities, they must be both consistent Christians and good parents. This means, first, that pastors must practice what they preach. John Pollock quotes Billy Graham's eldest son:

> History has shown that many public figures live two lives, one for the camera, the other behind closed doors. Not so with Mom and Dad. Their lives are the same before the public as they are behind closed doors.[10]

Consistently living out their faith in both public and private allows pastors to have spiritual leadership in their families:

■ I think of my dad as my spiritual father. He's very unusual. Most of the PKs I know are kind of frustrated with their parents. They don't see their parents in terms of spiritual leadership. But my dad does what he preaches.

Second, pastors must be good parents. Good parenting includes the ability to create the private "oasis" for one-on-one interaction with each child. This PK's father knew how to take a focused interest in her spiritual life:

■ I do very truly this day, and since I was in college, view my father as my spiritual father and my mentor. One thing he did for all of us, once we had graduated from high school, was to take us out to lunch or breakfast. Even today, whenever we gather for a weekend at our house, he and I will always have our one time alone for lunch together. Every time I would think, Okay, the big question is going to come when he'll lean across the table and say, "Now, Julie, where are you spiritually?" And I would have to answer! He's not trying to get a labeled answer, not trying to see how much you're leaping ahead. He's just curious to see where you're at. It is an important question that has made me think a lot. How significant it has been that he's asked me that!

Faith in Everyday Life

Some people, by contrast, seem to assume that parents in the ministry are automatically consistent Christians and good parents. If that is the case, then all PKs should have stable identities as Christians. Would those people be surprised to find out that many PKs are not Christians at all, or that the PKs did not personally acknowledge Jesus as Savior until after they had left their home church? Even if the pastor is not flagrantly hypocritical at home, he may nevertheless fail to imbue the home with the reality of faith in everyday life. Without this demonstration, the PK has much less than is needed on which to build a spiritual identity.

■ I have never seen my dad as a really religious person at home. I see him studying for his sermons once in a while, but for the most part when he's home, he's reading the paper, watching the news, reading a magazine, or reading a book. He didn't really talk about his beliefs or what his strong convictions are—what he thinks. He is a rather closed person to begin with—kind of quiet and keeping to himself.

I never joined the church. I don't know if that bothered my parents or not. I talked to my dad about it one time, and he said, "Son, I want you to do it if that's what you want to do. But please don't do it just to make me happy." My dad's happy to see me at church if I'm there. I'm rarely there.

On the one hand, it is commendable that the pastor wants his son to have an authentic rather than a forced commitment to the church. The son's faith decision should be truly his, not made to please the parents or the church. On the other hand, we must ask what would be the basis for the decision—a purely cognitive decision based on his father's sermons? Asking about joining the church may have been one way for the boy to discover his father's personal commitment and whether the church has any significance in his life beyond providing him with a job. The response instead leaves him still groping as to the depth of his father's faith.

In all fairness, we should not conclude on the basis of this PK's statements that the father has no authentic faith of his own. We must make allowances for *his* temperament, too; not to be openly expressive of his thoughts and emotions is not a sin. But we are left to wonder how all this looks from a child's perspective: If ministry seems little more than a job, what is church membership? If ministry is not the expression of a consistently lived faith, what is faith?

The boundary between the pastor's professional role and the family must not become a barrier between faith and family. Pastors, as Christian parents, have both the right and the responsibility to transmit a vital faith to their children. If moral dos and don'ts are to be passed on, it will happen because of the family's Christian commitments, not because of the minister's reputation:

> ■ If there is something you're telling your children they can't do, or you'd rather not have them do, make certain they understand it's because you're a Christian, not because you're a minister.

Parenting that demonstrates the realities of grace and forgiveness in everyday life provides a solid foundation for the child's spiritual life. In this vein, Paul Moody, the son of evangelist Dwight Moody, tells an illuminating story of his father. The boy was up past his bedtime, visiting with a friend who happened to drop by the Moody home. His father passed by and told Paul to go to bed. The son, not meaning to disobey, misread the command as meaning that he was to retire promptly when the friend left. Shortly afterward, Dwight Moody reappeared and repeated his command, this time much more forcefully. The son writes:

> This time I retreated immediately and in tears, for it was an almost unheard-of thing that he should speak with such directness or give an order unaccompanied by a smile. But I had barely gotten into my little bed before he was kneeling beside it in tears and seeking my forgiveness for having spoken so harshly. . . . Half a century must have passed since then, and while it is not the

earliest of my recollections I think it is the most vivid, and I can still see that room in twilight and that large bearded figure with the great shoulders bowed above me, and hear the broken voice and the tenderness in it. Before then and after, I saw him holding the attention of thousands of people, but asking the forgiveness of his unconsciously disobedient little boy for having spoken harshly seemed to me then and seems now a finer and a greater thing, and to it I owe more than I owe to any of his sermons. For to this I am indebted for an understanding of the meaning of the Fatherhood of God, and a belief in the love of God had its beginnings that night in my childish mind.[11]

Dwight Moody's tenderness toward his son may, in fact, have derived from similar treatment he received from his own father. Moody's oldest son, William, writes of his paternal grandfather's household:

In his home, grace was the ruling principle and not law, and the sorest punishment of a child was the sense that the father's heart had been grieved by waywardness or folly.[12]

Where grace reigns in the pastor's home, the wisdom of the parents is passed from generation to generation.

Models of Living Grace

Clergy parents who make their children feel important spend time with them, playing with them, talking to them, and showing interest in their activities. No matter how busy their schedules, these parents are always ready to provide a safe haven where the children can share whatever is going on in their lives.

The parents' focused attention, protected from the distractions of ministerial responsibilities, is an essential element in PKs' development of a positive sense of self. These parents show respect for their children as individuals with unique gifts and desires. The consistency of parental faith, at church and at home, is vital to the children's spiritual identity.

Does all this sound impossible to attain? It may be difficult—but not impossible. Ever and always, the goal is not to strive for perfection in ourselves, but to be made perfect in Christ. It bears repeating: Clergy should not be expected to be models of living perfection, but of living grace. If this is how they live their faith, they earn the freedom to fail with their children, even as they try in grace to grow as parents. For their part, the children will eventually realize that their parents are only human after all and that God is still worthy of their devotion.

NOTES

1. See, for example, the biography by David Ritz entitled *Divided Soul: The Life of Marvin Gaye* (New York: McGraw-Hill, 1985).

2. For a good introduction to the literature, see Henry B. Biller, *Paternal Deprivation: Family, School, Sexuality, and Society* (Lexington, Mass.: Lexington Books, 1974); and Michael E. Lamb, "Fathers and Child Development: An Integrative Overview," in *The Role of the Father in Child Development*, ed. Michael E. Lamb (New York: John Wiley, 1981), 1–70.

3. Michael E. Lamb, J. H. Pleck, and J. A. Levine, "Effects of Increased Paternal Involvement on Children in Two-Parent Families," in *Men in Families*, ed. R. A. Lewis and R. E. Salt (Beverly Hills: Sage Publications, 1986).

4. See, for example, Pauline Boss, "A Clarification of the Concept of Psychological Father Presence in Families Experiencing Ambiguity of Boundary," *Journal of Marriage and the Family* 39 (1977): 141–51.

5. John Pollock, *Billy Graham: Evangelist to the World* (San Francisco: Harper & Row, 1979), 139–41.

6. See Ivan Boszormenyi-Nagy and Geraldine Spark, *Invisible Loyalties* (New York: Harper and Row, 1973).

7. Jerry Falwell, *Strength for the Journey: An Autobiography* (New York: Simon & Schuster, 1987), 268.

8. Pollock, *Billy Graham*, 145.

9. Ibid.

10. Quoted in Pollock, *Billy Graham*, 139.

11. Paul D. Moody, *My Father: An Intimate Portrait of Dwight Moody* (Boston: Little, Brown, 1938), 82–83.

12. William R. Moody, *The Life of Dwight L. Moody* (New York: Fleming Revell, 1900), 24.

CHAPTER EIGHT

In-Groups
and Out-Groups

The characters in the drama of PK life include not only the children themselves and their parents, but also the PK's peer group. We have looked at PKs in terms of their inborn traits and sibling position. We have considered the parental influence through setting clear boundaries and making their children feel important. In this chapter we consider the role of peers in the development of a PK's sense of identity.

Let's consider a hypothetical family: the Smiths. One day a daughter—we will call her Bonnie—is born into the family. For the first few months, Bonnie's life is centered well within the confines of the Smith household. Indeed, her entire social world is mainly the duet between her and her mother or whoever has the primary task of caring for her needs. Gradually the circle widens, and other family members begin to figure prominently in Bonnie's life. For a few years, the most important part of her self-identity is created and sustained within her own family.

Then comes preschool or school. Bonnie's sense of worth is no longer based solely on her family's acceptance of her. She now becomes a public representative of the Smiths and must take her place alongside her peers in learning, performing, and producing. She begins to realize that she is being evaluated for how well she performs certain tasks, some of which come more easily than others. Quite naturally Bonnie begins to compare herself with her peers. How well the comparison goes depends on numerous factors: her capabilities, her emotional sensitivity, the sense of self-worth instilled by her family, the size of the group, and so on. Whatever the result, the ground of Bonnie's identity has begun to shift and widen.

The shift continues through adolescence, when Bonnie is approaching adulthood and is more self-consciously trying to fashion an identity of her own. Being a Smith may not seem as important as it once did. Bonnie has no doubt discovered that her parents do not have all, or even most, of the "answers," and she wants to make up her own mind about things. As she begins to look outside the family for guidance and options, for people to believe in and causes to follow, she finds that her friends are looking, too.

Bonnie and her friends tend to band into temporary groups and subgroups, united by a common activity or belief. The cement that bonds them may last anywhere from a day to many years. They draw an experimental sense of identity from whatever it is that holds them together. "We are the yearbook committee." "We party at Brian's house." "We smoke pot." "We will make the world a better place by. . . ." Being a group member gives Bonnie a feeling of belonging, and she may cling tenaciously to it. She may even go to extraordinary measures to preserve it. Peer support gives her the nerve to do things she would not do on her own. Alternately, of course, peer pressure also compels her to do things she would not do otherwise.

Eventually many of these peer groups disband. Friends who seemed knit together at the soul may drift apart. Relationships explode in anger or atrophy from neglect. When Bonnie has finished identifying with one group, she joins others, perhaps only to leave them again soon after. By late adolescence, Bonnie will retain some of her identifications and discard others. She leaves adolescence with a newly minted sense of her personal identity and enters adulthood making choices that will put her identity to the living test.

This scenario is, of course, a generalized and greatly oversimplified sketch of identity development. But whatever the details of a particular child's journey, the importance of the peer group cannot be brushed aside. A child's inborn characteristics and how parents deal with these are foundational to self-identity, but the family are not the only ones who build on the foundation.

FREEDOM TO MAKE CHOICES

For some parents, the day their children enter school is filled with anxiety. They realize that the kids are leaving the protective bubble of the family and are taking their first big step into the world beyond. Anxious parents snatch self-help books from store shelves, trying to find the magic formula that, if followed diligently, will guarantee successful, well-adjusted kids. But parents cannot control all of the variables that go into their children's lives. Children must eventually make choices of their own, and regardless of how much the parents have taught them, they sometimes make unwise choices. (Just as adults do!)

Parents, especially teenagers' parents, frequently fret over letting their children make choices. They especially worry about their choice of friends: Who are they spending time with? What do they do when they get together? Many anguished Christian parents relate stories of how their children chose friends who led them away from God, sometimes into lives of addiction or crime. There is nothing wrong with being appropriately concerned that children make the right choices. But sometimes the right choices can come only after someone makes a couple of wrong ones, as painful and damaging as that may be. And if the foundation for making the right choices has not already been laid, then a parent's continuing to control decisions from outside will not compensate for the child's missing internal "guidance system."

On the other side, it is hard for teenagers to understand what the parents are going through. Metaphorically, what if life were like a bicycle? Think of that magic moment when the training wheels are removed and children ride off down the street without any help. They may be anxious, but the exhilaration of doing it on their own drives them on. The parents, however, want to hold on to the seat, or at least run alongside for insurance! They want to protect their children from falling. But the time quickly comes when they must stop running, cross their fingers, and just watch as their children make their own way. The parents have to trust that their kids have learned enough balance to keep on course. Their job is no longer to make sure the children do not fall, but rather, to be there to help them if they do.

For clergy and their children, the situation can be a bit more complicated. The problem of living in a glass house again makes itself felt. When the PK's "training wheels" come off, so to speak, it may be the whole congregation that watches. One minister's son said his friends in the public school knew he was a PK, but it didn't seem to matter to them: "They knew my dad was a pastor, they knew that I had to go to church on Sunday, but they didn't have many expectations of me." The friends would invite him to parties or on trips, which meant missing church services now and then. This was not a problem for the congregation that his parents were serving at the time. But the PK stated emphatically that if it had been a previous church, when his family lived in a parsonage, "people would have put pressure on my parents" if he were to miss a Sunday. Thus, when it comes to peer groups and behavior, the watchfulness of the congregation can introduce restraints not experienced in nonclergy families.

Some PKs seem to make good choices from the start. To extend the metaphor, there are kids who seem to have a good sense of balance and receive the right amount of coaching from their parents, so that when the training wheels are off, they ride smoothly and surely along. Like this pastor's daughter, they choose friends and behaviors that are consonant with their parents' values:

> ■ I only had friends who didn't get into drinking and drugs. That was never a temptation for me. I remember that in my senior year I went to a party, looked around, and thought, "These people are just making fools of themselves. I don't want to do this."

Other pastors' kids may not be as strong at first. Perhaps they are off balance because their parents coached them too much, or perhaps too little. Whatever the reason, it does not help for all eyes to be on them, watching to see what happens.

WHY DOES EVERYONE TREAT ME AS IF I'M DIFFERENT?

This watchfulness includes the curiosity of the PK's peers. We have already seen that ministers' children are often expected to fit some oversimplified stereotypes, even in their peer group. When children are identified primarily as PKs, they are no longer just one of the crowd.

> ■ People constantly made remarks like "Well, you're a preacher's kid, and you're expected to do such and such." Not only adults, but also my peers. Once they found out I was a PK, their attitudes toward me changed.

Remember the minister's daughter's statement in chapter 4:

> ■ When we first moved to California, we attended a church near our home. The church had a lot of kids my age, and it was fun at first. Then everyone learned that my father was a minister looking for a new church to minister in, and I couldn't be me. I had to walk, talk, look, and breathe perfectly.

Friends may seem to be relating more to the stereotype than to the real person. These relationships have less to do with how PKs actually behave than with how friends *think* they must behave:

■ Peers of mine who swore would apologize repeatedly if they ever swore in front of me. No one ever expected that I too may swear occasionally. I was the perfect PK in their minds.

A story from Jim and Sally Conway about their daughter points out that a PK's schoolmates may on occasion be a bit tactless with their stereotypes:

Becki remembers an argument in school when a classmate challenged her to back up her point of view with a Scripture. Becki couldn't.

"You're a preacher's daughter," the girl sneered, "and you can't even quote the Bible."

"Well, your dad is a plumber," Becki retorted, "and you don't know how to fix pipes!"[1]

Peers are no different from adults in expecting ministers' children to be different from everyone else. And as most teenagers will tell you, it can be acutely embarrassing to stand out from the crowd. Even adults feel this at times. We want to know how people will dress for a certain occasion so that we don't come overdressed or underdressed. We may want to find out what kinds of gifts others are buying lest we spend too much or too little. The difference for teenagers is that they are less experienced with self-consciousness, and their self-identity may not be strong enough to resist the painful self-doubt that comes with being different.

PKs may also feel different if they don't get the same treatment their friends give everyone else. The differential treatment may be somewhat benign. The same PK who stated earlier that his friends at school didn't seem to care that he was a pastor's son found that unfortunately his church peers singled him out from the group:

■ I was seen as the pastor's kid, so they wouldn't involve me in certain types of activities. For example, sometimes they went to the movies and wouldn't ask me to go because they thought I wasn't supposed to go to movies. They would involve me in church activities, but in other things they would unintentionally leave me out.

We might well ask why it is all right for other kids in the church to go to the movies, but not the pastor's son. But whether or not this PK was allowed to go or wanted to go is beside the point: He was not given the opportunity. His perception is that his friends did not even think of asking him. And why not? Because he was the pastor's kid.

Breeding Resentment

At other times the treatment is much more intrusive, as friends pressure ministers' children in various ways. As we saw in chapter 4, PKs may be put in positions of authority or held up as examples to the other children in the church. Church members sometimes prod their children with questions like "Why can't you be more like the pastor's daughter/son?" This in turn can breed resentment in the PK's peers, and this resentment may be acted out in a number of ways.

One consequence of this vexation is competitiveness. A minister's daughter experienced what I call the "gunslinger" syndrome: In the Old West—at least in the Hollywood version—having a reputation as a "fast gun" virtually guaranteed facing one dusty showdown after another. This girl became "the one to beat":

■ There were many girls in church my age, and I felt I was the person they had to try to be better than and compete against. Yet I really wanted to do what I was doing without always being watched and being outdone or beaten in a way.

This PK may be honestly motivated to do her best in everything and have the talent to succeed in it. But how can she strive for excellence when she knows that all her peers are "gunning" for her? Competitiveness alone cannot sustain a relationship, and as long as her peers continue to single her out, it will be difficult for her to have honest friendships.

Feeling Guilty

There are other reasons why teens poke at the minister's kids. There is something about having a reputed "saint" around that brings out the devil in us. Teenagers are especially vulnerable as they try to sort out questions of values, belongingness, and identity. Let's face it: Good people make us feel guilty. And when we feel that way, it is hard to accept their behavior at face value. We want to detect their "real" motivations. We want to see them do something less than saintly. So peers may try to provoke and tempt ministers' children into transgressing some real or imaginary standard.

■ Because I lived in a reasonably small town, everyone knew who you were, that your dad was a pastor. This became a real problem in my later teens, when non-Christian guys started to take an interest in me. I could just feel everyone watching me to see what I would do and how I would react. This was also true when people started drinking, smoking, etc.—they knew I shouldn't, but they still really pressured me to, to see if I would give in.

Worse yet, PKs may be pushed back and forth between stereotypes, alternately being teased as a "goody-goody," then provoked to do something rebellious:

> ■ I was out with a bunch of guys one weekend night, and they decided to stop by a party. On the way, everyone was talking, and many of the words were swear words. Out of nowhere one of the guys turned to another and said, "Greg is just too good of a guy; he never swears." There were a couple of other PKs in my class, and they talked like everybody else, so these guys thought of me as a little saint. When we got to the party, they offered drinks to everyone, and most accepted, but I didn't. Someone there who knew my sister said, "She is a little rebel and drinks; what's wrong with you, you little goody-two-shoes?"

Even if the PK decided to have several drinks, the underlying problem would remain. It is not as if his friends would suddenly say, "Hey, I guess we were wrong about Greg. He's just a normal guy. Sorry, Greg!" Instead, he would now be labeled a rebellious PK. Either way, Greg has to live with being squeezed into a box instead of being accepted for who he is.

... BUT I *AM* DIFFERENT!

If there is difficulty in PKs' being treated *as if* they are different, there is greater hardship when they *are* different. Some differences may be counted as advantages, others as disadvantages. PKs' experiences can give them a view of life not shared by their peers. On the positive side, PKs may have a broader sense of world culture, having been exposed to missionaries and guests from various parts of the world or even having lived in other countries. Moreover, their experiences with people in the church have taught them important lessons about human nature that their friends may not learn for years. These factors, together with a constant exposure to a variety of adults, may give PKs a more mature outlook on life that distances them from others their age.

These potential advantages, if firmly embedded in a PK's experience, may significantly outweigh any disadvantages with respect to peers. But sometimes the awkwardness of being different feels burdensome, especially to peer-conscious teenagers. This may be especially true in denominations that forbid the activities that make up the social diet of their friends: rock music, dancing, movies, drinking, smoking, or wearing makeup. It is not that PKs necessarily want to do these things for any intrinsic value—they often have no idea what they are missing anyway. Rather, the rub comes in their not fitting in with the crowd. Everyone else can sing the number one song, but the PKs can't because they don't know it. Everyone else is abuzz with opinions on the big movie release of the summer, but the PKs haven't seen it. For them, it is almost like growing up in a different culture or speaking a different language; it is difficult to find common ground with their peers.

There is an additional source of confusion: If you look as if you should be the same as everyone else, it is more difficult for people to understand why you're not:

> ■ I do regret some of the cultural things that I didn't know because it still took me a very long time to come out and feel socially at ease. And I still feel very uncomfortable about getting into social situations; I never know if I'm going to say something wrong or make an assumption that's based on some script that I learned as a child growing up and that doesn't apply to now or this culture.
>
> There is something to be said for growing up in another culture when everybody knows it and forgives you. But to have grown up in a subculture where you *should* be like everyone else, and you're not—it's all inside, and your peers can't understand why you're different. Most of it is all inside, and when you can't meet expectations, you're not normal. . . . I am very tired of being different.

A World unto Itself

Part of the problem is that ministry is an all-absorbing way of life. First, there are *always* more ways to be involved in church life. The teenaged PK who wants to be involved can easily fill up the social calendar with church activities. Second, there are often expectations that PKs will be involved, and the more involved the better. Just as there are expectations of involvement for the parents, so there are for the children: participation or leadership in youth activities, clubs, and groups. Third—and positively—the opportunities for ministry can be an important source of self-identity for the PK, not just a requirement imposed from the outside.

These three factors, combined variably in different situations, make it easy for ministers' children to find themselves with little time or energy for the usual pursuits of adolescence:

> ■ I did what I could to be a part of "normal" social life, but frankly there was not always enough time to be both "normal" and a minister's daughter.

■ People could go to parties, and many times, because of the schedule or attending church, I didn't get a chance to do those things. Most of my activities were confined to church activities.

The all-absorbing nature of the ministry, however, is more than just a matter of how many hours there are in a day or a weekend. Ministry can be a whole world unto itself. Some ministers' children experience position, privilege, and responsibility in ways far beyond their peers. The ministry offers them a unique and valuable window into adulthood and a life of service. But the world that they experience may therefore be quite different from that of their peers. Communication becomes awkward:

■ My life was deeply embedded in my parents' work. It was very interesting to me, and I excelled in what I did: playing the piano, teaching Sunday school, and having a significant, respected role in worship services far before many kids are given that kind of respect. But it made it difficult for me to interact with kids my own age, who went to gymnastics, listened to rock music, and talked about hairstyles and boys. When I got together with friends, I found myself often bringing up my father's work, the different places I had lived as a result of his work, the way I thought about things because of his work. I received from my peers a kind of guarded interest in these stories, but they weren't really able to "join" with me and responded much more eagerly to other kids, who talked about the concert they had attended, etc.

I had to learn how to talk "superficially" with people and not to bring up my father's work as a topic of conversation. I am not sure whether I attribute all this discomfort with peers to my father's profession, but I think his profession contributed to my confusion about what the rest of the world was like.

Like other teenagers, pastors' children want to "fit in." It is uncomfortable and lonely being different. My wife and her sisters, for example, were raised in another land. When they came to this country, it was obvious that they looked and spoke differently from the other kids. Some of them were teased mercilessly; others were physically beaten on their way to or from school. The solution? Find a group to identify with. For my wife, the remedy came in the form of a small group of international students at her high school who had experienced similar embarrassment. Together they felt a sense of stability and sanity. The solution is much the same for many pastors' kids as they seek each other out on high school and college campuses.

■ The minister's family is never like any other—you are always an outsider. I have overheard guys in high school say, "I won't date her. She's a nice girl, but she's a preacher's kid." Not that I even cared for that person, but. . . . It hurt a little, but that's our story. We are different.

It is unfortunate that the simple phrase "She's a preacher's kid" can explain why a boy would refuse to ask a girl for a date. Did anyone ever respond, "So what?"

Fleeing Stereotypes

The feeling of wanting to fit in is the other side of the so-called rebellion in pastors' children. On the one hand, rebellious behavior can be a reaction against narrow stereotypes, as we saw in chapter 4. This is a movement away from the confinement that stereotypes impose on a PK's identity. On the other hand, such behavior may represent an equally strong pull toward the peer group, toward wanting to have a place among friends. The degree of rebellion, then, can be viewed from two directions. How strong are the stereotypes, the images of differentness, that PKs are trying to escape? And how great are the pressures of the peer group for PKs to behave in ways that the church would deem rebellious?

The most fortunate of pastors' kids do not experience significant pressure of either type. For others, the first kind of pressure may be the most important; for some, the second. And some may experience both:

> ■ One thing I struggled with in my teen years was fitting in with my peer group. I can remember that the guys at school constantly made remarks about my being a PK. That would make me only want to strive more just to fit in and prove myself. So I can remember getting involved with drinking, and smoking pot was a big thing—there wasn't anything stronger than that. As I reflect on it now, doing those things was an overt attempt to fit in, to not be different, to not be a PK, but to be just one of the guys.
>
> So in many ways, it was a real struggle for identity, wanting peer acceptance, and not wanting to be a PK. For me it was a dirty word to be a PK because of the view of my peers toward me.
>
> There was a stigma, too, attached to being a PK. People kind of expected you to be rebellious. That was the attitude in our church—and I think in other churches—that PKs tend to be rowdy and rabble-rousers. So I wanted to live up to that expectation—I didn't want to prove them wrong.

Some PKs, confronted with opposing stereotypes, find a way to eat their cake and have it too:

> ■ I wanted to be accepted by my peers because as a PK it was harder to be accepted. I went to parties and used to drink. I would only get tipsy, not drunk, and I didn't smoke or go out with guys.

So it was only mild rebellion, but I felt independent. I tried to form my own identity. I did this in the secular school, but at church I was still a perfect child.

Acceptance Is Where You Find It

Caught between the rock of unfair stereotypes and the hard place of intrusive expectations, teenaged PKs may have trouble finding acceptance anywhere among peers. If they do not find it in the church, they will look elsewhere. That sets the battleground for a major source of conflicts in clergy families—as in probably most Christian families—namely, the matter of friendships with non-Christians.

To PKs who have experienced rejection, it may seem that there is more grace outside the church than in:

> ■ I had many, many non-Christian boyfriends. Now I think I was so desperately trying to get affirmation, to feel okay about myself. So I did not want to go out with somebody who wanted to know whether you drink or smoke, and how many times you pray every day, and do you read your Bible, and did you have your devotions this morning, and all that. So I went out with people who smoked and drank, who would have slept with me if I would have let them. I've realized that that's where I first experienced some unconditional acceptance—from people outside. They didn't care that I was a PK.

How sad! Why is it that the first place where she felt accepted for herself, instead of her role, was outside the church? Is it any wonder that some PKs seem to have greater allegiance to non-Christian friends than to their peers in the church?

The solution is not simply to restrict PKs to having Christian friends, as if this would protect them from unfortunate decisions or undesired behavior. That does not always work:

> ■ We had an incredibly intense youth group. Everybody knew everybody's business; everybody was attached to everybody else. We all went to youth group on the weekend. And when you're in junior high, everything is "Are you going out with this boy?" or "Are you with this girl?" or "Do you like this person?" and "Oh, I think I like that person," or "I'm not sure; I don't know if he likes me." Being that age has got to be the worst! So what happened is that it started getting away from being a youth group and started becoming a dating scene, a social scene. And it got to the point more and more that the way I related to the guys, the way the girls in the group were friends with the guys, was to fool around with them, to get involved with them. That's when they would pay attention to you. . . .

> We'd all hang out and drink together. Some of the guys would
> hang out and get stoned together. That was our youth group.
> Sunday school—once a week for an hour, that was religiousness.
> But everybody was half-asleep anyway, kind of yawning, trying to
> peel their eyes open.

Apparently none of the adults in the church seemed to recognize that
any of this was happening. This is not meant as a portrait of the typical
neighborhood church youth group. But neither should clergy families
or other Christian parents ignore the realities of how many children
live.

The point is that we need to recognize the importance of peers
and the complicating factors that influence PKs' choices.

Moreover, none of what is said in this chapter should be
construed to mean that PKs should be allowed to do whatever they
please in the service of wrestling with their identity. Rather, we must
recognize the various roles that parents, other adults, and peers play in
the PK's drama of self-identity.

Clergy parents may find it difficult to recall their own struggles
with similar issues when they were teenagers. They may be too
preoccupied with the pressures of ministry to have much empathy with
their kids. An incident in the life of the medical missionary Albert
Schweitzer offers a poignant illustration of this. In his memoirs
Schweitzer, the young son of the village parson, tells how he tried to
bridge the gap between his family's social station and that of his lower-
class peers in the local village. He had gotten himself into a wrestling
match with a larger boy from the village, and Albert eventually won.
The victory was quickly soured, however, by the other boy's taunting
remark: "Yes, if I got broth to eat twice a week, as you do, I should be
as strong as you are." The comment pierced Schweitzer, for it
reminded him of

> what I had already been obliged to feel on other occasions: the
> village boys did not accept me as one of themselves. I was to them
> one who was better off than they were, the parson's son, a sprig of
> the gentry.[2]

Young Albert tried to be like the other boys however he could,
especially in the way he dressed. He preferred to wear more ragged
clothing than he was accustomed to so that he would fit in with his
peers—much to the consternation of his parents. His mother would
tolerate his clothes to spare him the unkind remarks of others. Albert's
father, however, would confine him to the cellar or box him on the ear.
The issue of clothing, which seems to have had great symbolic

importance for both Albert and his father, became a continual source
of conflict between them.

> Every time a visitor came the contest was started afresh, for it was
> my duty to present myself dressed "suitably to my station in life."
> Indoors, indeed, I yielded in every way, but when it was a case of
> going out to pay a visit dressed as a "sprig of the gentry," I was
> again the intolerable creature who provoked his father, and the
> courageous hero who put up with boxes on the ear and let himself
> be shut up in the cellar. . . . The village boys never knew what I
> went through on their account; they accepted without emotion all
> my efforts not to be in any way different from them, and then,
> whenever the slightest dispute arose between us, they stabbed me
> with the dreadful words, "sprig of the gentry."[3]

The experiences Schweitzer describes occurred in the late
nineteenth century, but the same kinds of tensions persist today. It is
still quite common to find a disparity of social class between clergy
families and their congregations. Many clergy have more education,
yet less income, than the average church member. These are real
differences that affect the lifestyle and outlook of the pastor's children.
And the children may feel these differences as barriers to acceptance in
their peer groups. Consider that a lower income may mean that the
minister's family cannot afford the same kind of clothing that the other
kids wear. Clothing, as it was for the Schweitzer family, is still an
important status symbol, especially among adolescents. Some PKs
remember their mothers' having to sew their clothes but being
sensitive enough to try to make them fashionable. These mothers
knew, as did the children themselves, how important it can be to fit in.

DO WE HAVE TO MOVE *AGAIN?*

Another experience common to pastors' children that sets them
off from most of their peers is frequent moving. Most PKs move at
least a couple of times before reaching adulthood, and many move
much more often than that. Leaving one community for another means
abandoning what may be a carefully constructed network of friends,
especially but not exclusively in the case of teenagers. These
friendships can define an important part of the adolescent PK's
personal identity. It is no wonder that some ministers' children resist
moving to another community.

The reactions of teenagers may range from a passive and
withdrawn acceptance to raging resistance. In part that has to do with
the way the decision to move is made; that is, whether the PKs feel as
if their needs and opinions are taken into account. This PK rates the

dislocation caused by moving as the most perplexing problem of being in a clergy family:

> ■ The biggest factor in our differences of adjustment and acceptance of being PKs was our ages during big moves and our peer groups who accepted or rejected us.

Frequent moving makes it impossible to establish a stable peer network that can be relied on to support the PKs' identity-building explorations. To compensate, they may have to rely more on their parents and other adults for emotional sustenance.

> ■ Moving a lot made me self-sufficient, that is, less dependent on peers for approval and perhaps more dependent for emotional support and affirmation on my family. My strategy was to please the dominant authority figures in my life (parents and teachers) and to ignore or insulate myself from peer evaluations.

The quirk in this statement is that what the PK calls self-sufficiency is really a shift in the basis of sufficiency from peers to family. Although this need not be a problem in itself, it does give a different direction to identity development. This is especially a problem for PKs in clergy families that are dysfunctional in some way. Becoming more dependent on one's family, at a time when most other teenagers are becoming less dependent, may mean missing or delaying important opportunities to create a more securely self-sufficient identity. And when the family itself has problems, the PK may feel locked up, with no escape. This PK, who was born to "perfectionistic and workaholic" parents, laments feeling unimportant because of what moving did to her social network:

> ■ The ministry pulled us out of schools in midyear, separated us from friends, and isolated us as a semi-functional family at best.

CONCLUSION

The stage of a PK's life is densely populated. Parents, congregations, and peers can push and pull ministers' children in different directions. The children themselves have the delicate task of creating a viable sense of identity in the midst of expectations and stereotypes. We can make it easier by relaxing the pressures we may unwittingly place on them. One way is to recognize that the need to fit in with peers can be very strong. We can realize how important friends are to their identities when it comes to making decisions about moving. Even if we can identify with their feelings, however, we must not over-identify with them. This is part of respecting them as individuals in their own right.

We should not force our own solutions on PKs prematurely; they must discover on their own. To return to the metaphor of the bicycle, we need to coach PKs in ways that are appropriate to how they learn as individuals. Our coaching affects the outcome. Some need the training wheels on longer; others, barely at all. If we deride the children for falling down, we erode their self-confidence and make it that much more likely that they will fall down again. And if we keep telling them that they cannot make it without the training wheels, they will either believe us or else grab a wrench and take the wheels off themselves.

If PKs have truly been raised with grace, that grace will see them through. If they have not, it is never too late to start.

NOTES

1. Jim and Sally Conway, "What Do You Expect from a PK?" *Leadership* 5 (1984): 84.

2. Albert Schweitzer, *Memoirs of Childhood and Youth*, trans. C. T. Campion (New York: Macmillan, 1950), 9.

3. Ibid., 11.

CHAPTER NINE

The Saints Below

We have looked at the roles played by PKs, their parents, and their peers in the drama of identity in the lives of ministers' children. One more group of players is needed to round out the cast: the parishioners.

Some of the classic hymns of the church celebrate the oneness of the earthly church with the heavenly church in rhapsodic tones. The well-known hymn "O for a Thousand Tongues," for example, contains this seldom-used stanza:

> Glory to God and praise and love
> Be ever, ever given
> By saints below and saints above,
> The Church in earth and heaven.

Another hymn, "Come, Let Us Tune Our Loftiest Song," makes a similar exhortation:

> Burn, every breast, with Jesus' love;
> Bound, every heart, with rapturous joy;
> And saints on earth, with saints above,
> Your voices in His praise employ.

Some people find such boundless praise difficult, tempered as it is by skepticism about the "saints below." A modern wit created this more popular rhyme:

> To dwell above with saints we love,
> Oh, wouldn't that be glory!
> To dwell below with saints we know—
> Well, that's another story!

We have referred often in earlier chapters to the influence of church members on PKs in terms of boundaries, stereotypes, and expectations. In this chapter we will emphasize two issues that commonly affect how pastors' kids experience congregations: the use and abuse of power, and the prevalence of hypocrisy in the church.

As Jack Balswick and I argue in *Life in a Glass House,* the congregation is a unique work setting in that it often functions emotionally much as a family does.[1] Indeed, many PKs speak of the congregations their parents serve as their "extended families." This, again, is part of what distinguishes the lives of pastors' children from others'. In most families, the people whom parents serve professionally have little or nothing to do with the children and have negligible influence on identity development. Clergy families, however, are embedded in the larger family of the church, and parishioners may exert considerable influence on the development of the children's sense of self.

Like real families, church members sometimes fight and bicker with one another. Disputes can arise over the most minor of matters, the gossip and criticism begin to fly, and the battle lines are drawn. William Hulme writes:

> The congregation is like a big family and, like biological families, can sometimes be racked with dissension. Churches as well as denominations repeatedly present a sad spectacle with their destructive intrafamilial feuding.[2]

Hulme explains these conflicts as a natural result of the more familial atmosphere:

> The congregation is a convenient projection screen for all the individual frustrations its members experience outside the congregational community. Its organizational structures are a tempting setting for the power plays and the control games so often blocked elsewhere by the impersonal structures of our society.[3]

So congregations frequently act like feuding families as church members use the church to take out their frustrations. Sometimes the feuding takes the form of open schisms; other times it is manifested more passively, in comments made behind people's backs. But whatever the form, all this can mean increased expectations on the clergy family.

The question is, what do PKs think when they see this kind of conflict? Does it affect them at all, and if so, how? After all, here they are, expected to be sterling examples of sainthood while all around them the rest of the saints may be in complete turmoil!

The chaos of emotions that characterizes some congregations can be extremely confusing to the pastor's children. "Why do people act like that?" they may wonder. "What are they so mad about? Why do they treat us this way—what did we do? Why don't they like me?" The children may then turn to their parents for answers. Some clergy appear well equipped to deal with such questions and can answer them fairly and openly in terms appropriate for the children. Other clergy parents, however, are less helpful; they may ignore or refuse to answer the questions, use the questions as an opportunity to lash out at the congregation, or simply feel lost and confused themselves. This minister's daughter speaks for many as she describes being fed up with the unreasonable demands of congregations and the confusion of a child trying to make sense of it all:

■ If there is any single reason that I struggle with going to church or having anything to do with organized religion, it is that I cannot tolerate one more ounceful of the petty, insipid, stupid demands that parishioners place on the minister. Part of what I consider pettiness does have something to do with people criticizing my father. I know I felt protective of him, in part because I adored my father and wanted all of what I considered his goodness to be mine. But it wasn't just a blind kind of protectiveness that I felt (and still feel). I myself have been critical of my father and, in spite of my idealization of him, have had an honest enough relationship, that I think I can see his shortcomings. The kind of criticism that angered me the most was the kind that had no basis in reality. It came simply from someone having a need for power or affirmation or attention or whatever, not getting that need met, and then out of the hurt blaming my father or both my parents. My parents didn't know how to respond to this with empathy, good boundaries, or a lack of personalization. And believe me, as a child, that kind of interpersonal configuration is bewildering, hurtful, enraging, and almost confusing enough to cover the face of God.

Many PKs report that they have witnessed little or no pettiness, power plays, or hypocrisy. Others, however, are still hurting from the last time they felt bruised by church members.

CONFLICT IN THE CHURCH

Some disputes among church members can reach the point of dividing the church into warring factions. But what do they fight about? We might sentimentally imagine that divisions usually arise from religious commitment—disagreements over doctrine and articles of the faith. In fact, again and again in the history of the church, whole new denominations have been born out of doctrinal dissent. But what pastors' children are more likely to see in the day-to-day life of the church are petty disputes. In some congregations, parishioners seem to have a knack for turning congregational decisions into monumental struggles. To the PK, some of the arguments seem downright silly and blown far out of proportion:

> ■ Some people would get caught up in the most nit-picky of things I have ever seen. If something wasn't right, they would almost go crazy over it, even if a table or something wasn't where they thought it should be put.

Ministers' children who have the opportunity to observe the official decision-making process may be quite disillusioned by what they see:

> ■ One incident that stands out in my mind was the year I was the youth group president and proudly attended my first official board meeting. The board was not particularly on their best behavior that night. The discussion among people I had considered "saints" raged for over an hour and was heated enough to produce name-calling and nearly came to blows—over, of all things, the color of the new sanctuary carpet! I was so angered and distressed by what I had witnessed that I refused to attend another meeting.

Life-and-death conflicts over petty issues like this leave some PKs wondering about the church's priorities. To them, the strife represents abandonment of the church's true purpose:

> ■ I could write a book on my experiences on this subject. Many people tend to get upset over the little things associated with churches, such as carpet color, program types, and taking the offering before Communion or after. These are just a few of the hundreds of petty complaints I witnessed at church during my lifetime. It seems many people forget the purpose of the church and the true gospel message presented by Christ.

It is not just a matter of *what* congregations fight over, but also *how*. The church becomes the arena for parishioners to play politics behind the scenes, fall into schisms, and act aggressively toward each other:

> ■ I knew a woman who would call certain members of the church to get what she wanted. I knew of the prospect of adultery between two church members. This later caused a split indirectly. I knew about the board meeting that became a boxing match between two of its members.

Such antics seem to occur less frequently in churches led by fair and determined pastors. Some pastors seem gifted by God to provide loving leadership:

■ I don't recall witnessing much pettiness or power plays in the church. My dad was very much in control of the church body—not in a dictatorial way, but as a strong leader. He was able to settle any disputes in a fair, calm fashion. He practiced equality, and therefore I believe members of the congregation felt important and needed in the proper functioning of the church.

■ My father had a unique blend of firm conviction and a loving spirit. This combination seemed to make him a peacemaker. At two different churches my peers told me that their folks had said that the church had never been healthier or had a better sense of unity and purpose than under my father's ministry.

The minister's ability to project calm, warmth, and firmness seems crucial. But even with wise guidance, parishioners may continue to bicker and fight. This minister's daughter obviously loves and admires her father, but she is critical of the congregation's apparent immaturity:

■ Why does everyone want to be the leader? It's not all it's cracked up to be. It is demanding, exhausting, and not glamorous. My dad is a very wise man who never acts in self-interest. He can get a totally unbiased perspective on a situation. So the only thing I am left to wonder is, why can't other men be so wise? Some of them are spiritual babies, really.

THE ABUSES OF POWER

The in-fighting between the "saints below" can leave PKs feeling bewildered. But what truly hurts them is when the clergy family itself is victimized by the way power is wielded in the church. This is particularly true in denominations that provide for congregations to vote whether to retain or dismiss the minister. When the date of the decision draws near, clergy families may become anxious, waiting to see if the ax will fall. It can be a particularly stressful time for the children, who do not know until after the decision is made whether or not they will have to move to a new community, attend a different school, and develop a whole new set of friends. Their fate, it seems, is in the congregation's hands—and they may already know the congregation to be capricious and unpredictable where important decisions are concerned.

Sometimes the decision comes as a complete shock, as when the pastor has been dismissed as the result of a seemingly arbitrary assertion of power. The pain and disillusionment can be tremendous for the entire family:

■ My father was victim to two major power plays in his pastoral career. One caused him to leave the ministry for several years, and the other almost caused him to leave the ministry altogether. These two events have left emotional scars on our entire family. My dad arrived at church one Sunday, and the leadership told him that he was released from his duties. I will never forget the pain my family felt when my dad was "fired," and seeing the disappointment in my parents as they hugged on the road after the decision. This hug seemed endless, and so does the pain. Many people in the church, including leaders, have forgotten the saving and *loving* message taught by Christ, especially when trying to meet their own human objectives.

Wherever power resides, there is the potential for the abuse of it. The fact that a congregation may have the authority to vote the pastor out does not give license for an insensitive handling of the decision. Wouldn't anyone else in the congregation be deeply hurt if he or she showed up to work one day, only to be told, "You're fired"? There is no problem with a legitimate exercise of authority. Ideally, if a congregation is not satisfied with a pastor's performance, the pastor should have already been counseled of this, and a mutually agreeable solution should have been worked out. Eventually, if matters still cannot be resolved, a dismissal may be required, but it should be handled with due compassion for the pastor's family.

Too often, clergy families simply feel they are dispossessed without just cause. Feeling victimized by the congregation, PKs may develop feelings of mistrust toward parishioners. When Jonathan Edwards was dismissed from a Massachusetts church in 1750, the family had nowhere else to go immediately and was obliged to stay in the area for more than a year. His daughter Esther was deeply hurt and learned not to trust what to her seemed to be the whims of a congregation:

> When Esther was eighteen, her father was dismissed from his Northampton pastorate. Over a year later the family moved to Stockbridge. The humiliation of the dismissal, the awkwardness of remaining for sixteen months where one was no longer wanted, and the exile to a dangerous frontier was traumatic for Esther. She acquired a distrust of the capriciousness of congregations and an acute sensitivity to the precarious position of a clergyman (and his family) totally dependent on his ability to please his parishioners.[4]

Many ministers' children confront these same feelings today: bitterness and betrayal.

> ■ These people had the power to change everything in my life, to turn it upside down. And many times they did. After we were in a particular church for a time, the congregation would vote you out. . . . I came to doubt every person in the church. I became distrustful of everyone and just expected that everyone would

reject me at some time or another. I still have to fight feelings of mistrust.

■ My younger sister is struggling right now with the idea that there isn't a God, or if there is, he is cruel. The reason for this is that my father was asked to resign from two churches. In the process all trust my sister had for people was stripped away.
I know that my father had done nothing to deserve that. Since that time my father has been struggling with his health. My sister is very rebellious and yet still goes to church, but just out of ritual.

■ Three churches I have been a part of forced my family to leave. At one church they stopped paying us—the starvation theory. At another the congregation started rumors that my father was having an affair. In a small town, news travels, and when you are already the outsider you lose hands down. Often I had to ask to get the full story. I could never understand why the people didn't like us (me). In several instances the very people I trusted the most in the congregation stabbed my family the worst. I stopped talking to congregation people about anything. I knew nothing as far as they were concerned.

Why were the fathers of these children asked to leave? On the one hand, the dismissals appear to the PKs to be based on malice or caprice, backed up with artificial rationalizations. On the other hand, the boards, if asked, would no doubt have offered some reasonable justification for their decisions. Children may not fully understand the reasons why a pastor is forced to resign. But although the fairness of the decision itself is an important issue, so is the way the decision is reached and then delivered. For PKs and their families, perhaps what hurts the most is to have people they trusted become instrumental in their removal. The feeling of betrayal cuts to the core. Children may not understand all the ins and outs of church politics, but they know whether or not they have been treated with compassion.

The Multiple Staff

Yet congregations are not the only ones who hold power. Where there is more than one pastor on staff, there is frequently a tangible hierarchy of power. Associate pastors may serve under a senior pastor who wields authority like a stick. In the end, of course, it is the associate who loses the power struggle, and the family feels victimized:

■ I have witnessed the manipulation of people in a number of churches my dad pastored. Sadly, the most obvious one was by the senior pastor of a church my dad was an associate pastor for. Whenever a ministry was successful and "producing fruit," the senior pastor would begin to put dampers on the program, move to phase it out; eventually, out of frustration the person or minister in charge would resign and leave. In a case where a minister was persistent and determined to keep his ministry, the senior pastor and some of his "groupies" went as far as to spread false rumors and accusations that led to ultimate disgrace and embarrassment for the pastor's family and friends. My dad tried to confront the senior pastor on many occasions to defend his colleague, and that led to my father's dismissal as well.

■ In one church, there was a very overpowering senior pastor. He decided to leave the church and start up a new one, but he made sure that he still had some minor hold on the church. My father was left in charge. Everything was going well, and the church began to grow rapidly, when this certain pastor that left decided that the church was not being run properly, so he promptly returned and snatched back his position, after saying some extremely cutting things to my dad. We decided to leave the church. This happened some time ago, and now it's really sad to hear the news that the church has severely decreased in numbers and is said to be collapsing.

This is sad indeed. The church as a human organization can be so infected by power games and striving for position that it remains *only* a human organization instead of functioning as the body of Christ. Faced with worldly politicking and manipulation, many PKs learn to be wary of giving their trust.

WHOM CAN I TRUST?

Why should PKs be trusting? From their vantage point, they see a great deal of hypocrisy in the church: people who say they are Christians yet behave in very un-Christian ways. From the rank and file all the way to the pinnacle of church leadership, PKs see people who profess and then profane the faith.

■ The people would sit in the pew on Sunday and live like a terror Monday through Saturday. I witnessed adultery, theft, demon-possession, back-stabbing, etc.

Sometimes the hypocrisy they see is in their own peer group:

■ I see a lot of my friends at youth group act very spiritual and then gripe about people behind their backs. Others do worse things.

Or among the church staff:

■ In high school, I became aware of infidelity among the deacons and of lots of other personal tragedies.

■ The hypocrisy I saw was more with the leaders and church staff—a lot of back-stabbing or dealing under the table with certain issues.

■ There was another minister, who was a hypocrite. He hated the church, worked on the side, but smiled every Sunday. It's no wonder his kids turned out the same way. Perhaps this contributes to my ambivalence. I'm not set against the church, but I'm waiting to see a good one.

The prevalence of hypocrisy varies, of course, from church to church. One PK recalls only a few instances but suspects there was more that he never saw:

■ I witnessed some hypocrisy among a few individuals in the churches, but on the whole I saw very little. I'm sure much more hypocrisy existed outside the realm of my vision. I lost all respect for the hypocrites I saw. Their faith to me seemed worthless and ungenuine.

Others have seen so much that they take it to be the standard of church life. The lack of consistency can sour them on the church, and it affects their own identity as Christians:

■ Terrible hypocrisy! I learned very early in life the difference between Christians dedicated to the Lord and those who were dedicated to everything else first.

■ Hypocrisy runs rampant in any church. Everybody is a hypocrite to some extent. This was a massive turn-off to me. I hated Sunday school. I felt judged negatively there. I feel this way at college too: Everybody is so fake.

■ I saw a great deal of hypocrisy in the church. In fact, I must say that I saw very little "realness" in the lives of most church people. Attendance and involvement seemed far more important than genuineness. And that's what I learned, too. Christianity, in my years of childhood and youth, was doing and obeying rules and religious ways, far more than it was knowing God in a personal and meaningful relationship.

■ I saw lots of hypocrisy in the church, and it sickened me. I became bitter, angry, and resentful about people in the church because of things they did to Mom, Dad, and our family. It disillusioned my faith in people, and I have difficulty trusting and developing close relations with others in the church because I know their capability to hurt.

So the "sad spectacle" of which William Hulme speaks includes petty bickering, capricious uses of power, and hypocritical behavior of church members and staff. Churches manifesting these problems have them in varying combinations and different degrees. The important issue is how these faults affect the identity of clergy children, especially their spiritual identity. To what extent does the spiritual health of a congregation account for differences among PKs in regard to faith?

CHRISTIANITY BEGINS AT HOME

All one-dimensional explanations are too simplistic to do justice to the PK's social environment. To be sure, the behavior or misbehavior of parishioners is an important factor in a PK's faith development. Ministers' children can become cynical and ambivalent about the church. Others, however, testify that hurtful experiences have strengthened their faith. What makes the difference?

Many factors enter in. Individual traits account for some of the differences. One pastor's child may be more sensitive to the thoughts and feelings of others and will be more strongly affected by pettiness and hypocrisy than a sibling who is somewhat aloof. Another factor is whether or not the PKs find some fitting role models of faith in the congregation:

> ■ I found hypocrisy in my church as well as anywhere else, but I don't feel that it affected my faith a whole lot because the people whom I looked up to were strong in their faith.

By far the most important factor, however, seems to be the way clergy parents deal with such matters. PKs who are generally able to take these experiences in stride are shown to have parents who are able to communicate effectively and openly, who demonstrate a consistency of faith in word and deed. These children learn not to equate Christianity with the behavior of errant church members.

Understanding Human Nature

What do these clergy parents teach their children? First, they use problems in the church to teach practical lessons about fallible human nature. They try to help the children distinguish their attitudes toward God and church from their attitudes toward parishioners:

> ■ My parents talked to us quite a lot and helped me to understand human nature.

> ■ They wanted us to realize that the church is a good place; it's just that people are human and aren't always going to get along.

> ■ My parents would explain that every person is responsible for his or her relationship with the Lord and that I shouldn't let someone else's affect mine.

■ Mom and Dad warned us that some people would let us down and make mistakes. They told us that the only one who wouldn't let us down is the Lord. Our eyes should be on him as a guide for our Christian life, not on other people.

These parents also teach the children the importance of being consistent and honest:

■ My parents taught me that my outside appearance should reflect my inner self, that God respects those who live up to what they claim to be.

■ My parents taught me to live what I believe.

As a result of such counsel, many ministers' children are able to see hypocrisy and pettiness in the congregation without its jeopardizing their faith. They learn not to reduce Christianity to the behavior of Christians:

■ I saw quite a bit of hypocrisy. I don't feel it affected my faith, but only my attitude toward the people.

■ I saw a lot of hypocrisy, but I just blame people for their problems, not God or the church.

■ What congregations did turned me off in a big way from church and ministry, but not so much from Christianity.

PKs with thoughtful parents understand that each person is responsible for his or her own behavior. In some cases, the PKs' faith in God has become stronger as their faith in people has diminished:

■ My parents always tried to teach the "right" thing to do in alignment with the gospel. Because of the obvious hypocrisy in the church, my faith was strengthened. Mankind should never put faith in man, but rather in God. I recognize that we have serious weaknesses as men, and I must always be on guard to reduce the risk of hypocrisy.

■ I soon learned that it didn't matter about others and their relationship or lack of relationship with God—it was my relationship with God that counted. I learned to stop looking at others. Looking at others means your eyes are on people instead of God, and you turn away from God pretty quickly.

Instead of focusing on others' misdeeds, these PKs learn to evaluate themselves more honestly and to be less judgmental of others:

■ My dislike of this has helped me to just be honest about my life and feelings. I'm very accepting of all people even if I don't approve of their lifestyles. It's not my job to judge. As Christians, we are to accept others even if we don't like their way of living.

■ While I am sure there was some hypocrisy, I was not aware of much. What I did see did not affect my faith. I recognized that we are a fallen people, and I knew that I wasn't perfect.

■ It actually increased my faith in God, and I became more aware of my own hypocrisy.

■ It made me want to live a God-pleasing life so that the non-Christians around me would know that not all people claiming to be Christians are hypocrites—or perfect either.

It would seem, then, that when clergy parents intervene to teach their children honestly and realistically about human nature, grace, and sin, PKs are able to weather congregational storms.

Does verbal instruction alone meet this goal? Probably not. More important, perhaps, than *what* clergy parents teach is *how* they teach it. Ministers' children need to see their parents modeling what they teach. When this happens, PKs have a solid example to follow that helps them put parish difficulties in a proper perspective. These are parents who practice what they preach.

■ At the time, you want to totally rebel, but then, you see, *you* would be the hypocrite. In a way, I look to my dad as an example, as he never (or very rarely) does hypocritical things, and I want to be like him in that way.

■ My parents never verbally addressed the issue of hypocrisy to me. Their teaching was by example. They lived their lives according to their values and morals. We were expected to live the same lifestyle and set the same sort of example.

■ I came to realize that all people are imperfect and have flaws. My parents were pretty consistent with their lives. I feel very fortunate that I had two wonderful parents while growing up.

Parents who live out their faith instill faith, compassion, forgiveness, and reconciliation:

■ My parents were incredibly strong through these times. It was evident that they trusted in the Lord. They explained that we were in the ministry for a reason, that in everything there will be opposition or things that don't seem right, but we were in the ministry, and the Lord hasn't sent us any place different.

■ My parents handled problems in the church with outstanding displays of forgiveness and acceptance after initial pain and sorrow.

■ My parents were often hurt, but they talked with the people in an effort to solve things and worked hard at reconciliation.

■ My parents taught me a lot by example. When people treated my parents badly, they didn't lash back at them and treat them badly in return. They told me many times to "do unto others as you will have them do unto you." This was a very good example for me to follow in my own life.

The other side of this matter is the damaging effect of hypocrisy that occurs in the clergy home. Pastors' kids cannot resolve the difficulties they see and experience in the congregation when their families are no better. Their spiritual identity suffers:

■ Lots of hypocrisy—especially at home. I saw so much that was unreal that it caused a period of rebellion in my late teens. There were good times and times of genuine spirituality, but the lack of consistency turned me off.

■ I saw very little hypocrisy in other people, but *heaps* in my own home. I've reacted, quite the opposite, where I tend to withdraw from ministering if I sense there is anything in my life that's not right, which is just as wrong.

Regardless of problems with the congregation, it is clear that faith begins at home. Clergy parents teach their children by both what they say and what they do.

Defining Boundaries

Parents also mediate the effects of parishioner behavior on their children by defining the boundaries between the family and the church. As we saw in chapters 2 and 7, clergy parents' personal boundaries must be secure enough to recognize where their responsibilities end and the parishioners' begin. Speaking of pettiness and abuses of power in the congregation, one PK remarked:

■ I think both were evident in the church as I grew up. My parents handled them well, with the right amount of involvement, knowing that they needed to be a part of the solution, but not all of it.

When boundaries are too fluid, clergy parents let their frustrations spill over into the family, invoking similar feelings in their children. One PK wrote that his parents were always critical of the congregation, which was "a big thing I had to discard as I grew older." Another minister's son reported how his parents' attitudes defined his own:

■ We were often told, indirectly, what to think about the conflicts. Church members were stereotyped for us by our parents' reactions. I'll confess to spreading gossip. I even called one son of a "troublemaker" a "secular kid" to his face. He didn't understand, but was offended.

Parents who draw fairly rigid boundaries shield their children from church problems:

■ The parents kept these things behind closed doors, and I had left home by the time I really became aware of these difficulties.

This protection depends on the children's level of awareness. Clergy parents may believe that they are protecting their children for their own good, without realizing that the kids are already quite aware of the problems and may need some help understanding them.

■ Sometimes they would explain a little, but usually we were just left to wonder about all the stuff we heard, legitimately or otherwise.

■ Most times, when I was younger, I just observed most things, often wondering why someone had left the church. I guess my parents thought they were protecting me. Even as an older teenager I observed many things and asked Mom. (Dad felt as though we didn't need to know.) Basically I didn't know why people left. One experience, which led us to leave the town and church, was explained a little bit by Mom, but I know there's still lots I don't know about the situation.

■ I don't think my parents realized how much we kids knew what was happening, so they didn't explain much. Perhaps they would have, had they known how much I picked up!

■ As a child growing up I always knew more than people gave me credit for. My parents felt it was better that I didn't know everything. But I knew just enough that I could draw the proper picture.

Some clergy parents are more willing to discuss congregational matters with their children, but here, too, there are differences of degree. Some only discuss matters that the children ask about or think the children *need* to know:

■ Dad always felt (and still does) that as pastor, God has given him and Mom the strength to deal with problems in the church, but that's no reason to dump them on us. So they protected us as much as possible from pettiness and power plays. Of course, at times such things were obvious, and then if we asked about them, Mom would try to explain.

If not saying anything holds risks, it is harmful at the other extreme to tell children too much:

■ It was always a problem for me to know too much. I wasn't always responsible with my information or my attitudes.

The key is whether or not the children themselves feel left in the dark. Clergy parents should be able to discuss problems openly but *in*

ways that are appropriate to their children's curiosity and knowledge. This
is analogous to the "big" question that many parents dread: the day a
child asks how he or she was born. One is reminded of the joke about
the little boy who came to his father and asked, "Daddy, where did I
come from?" His father took a deep breath and launched into a long
and detailed lecture about reproduction. Finally, when his father
finished, the boy wrinkled his nose and said, "Oh! Well, Tommy says
that he came from Cleveland."

That father could have saved himself a lot of trouble by first
finding out what the child really wanted to know. Children vary greatly
in their level of curiosity and in what they count as a sufficient
explanation. The parents' own anxiety about the question should not
compel them either to overload the children or to fail to satisfy the
quest for understanding.

For our purposes, the topic may be different, but the principle is
the same. Ministers' children may see a great deal of unsaintly
behavior in the congregation and need help in understanding it. Some
children are more curious than others, and some are more troubled by
what they see. Clergy parents should take these differences into
account when explaining matters to their children. Explaining issues
about which children are not curious is not helpful:

> ■ Most of the time, things were well explained, but at times I was
> not interested and was very confused about it all.

Children must be helped to understand in ways that respect their
individual boundaries. Parents, for example, may tailor their explanations according to the PKs' ages, entrusting them with more details as
they get older:

> ■ When I was younger, they explained things to me in general
> terms, but I really had little understanding. Once in high school,
> however, they talked pretty freely with me about these situations.

Remember the PK who attended his first board meeting? The board
members nearly had a fist fight over the color of the new carpet, and
the PK refused to return. The story has a positive conclusion. The
youth's parents discussed it with him and with the board in a way that
preserved his boundaries. The matter was resolved appropriately:

> ■ My parents and I talked about it several times. They tried to
> help me understand but allowed me to make my own decision.
> When the next meeting came and I was not in attendance, a
> member asked my father where I was. He said there was a
> shocked silence at his calm reply—and then some very embar-
> rassed faces—and they said, "Tell him it'll never happen again."

Dad's reply was great: "Maybe you should tell him." Believe it or
not, they did—they apologized, and I went back to the meetings.
Needless to say, we all learned a valuable lesson on that one!

The parents respected the boy's boundaries in two ways. First, having
discussed the matter thoroughly, they trusted him to make his own
decision. Second, instead of acting as his son's representative, the
pastor refused to be the go-between and encouraged the board to
apologize directly to the boy. The combination between appropriate
explanation and respect for boundaries made for a positive learning
experience for all. The point is that when PKs feel they need sensitive
situations explained, they can rely on their parents to help them:

> ■ My parents did explain things to me if they felt it was necessary.
> If I asked, they were always willing to answer. When I was
> younger, I probably didn't realize some of the things that were
> going on. When the church split a couple of years ago, I was fully
> aware of what was going on, and Mom and Dad also explained
> things to us, which was great of them.

FOR BETTER OR FOR WORSE

Because the congregation is like an extended family to the
pastor's children, members can influence PKs either positively or
negatively. When congregations are supportive and expectations are
appropriate, pastors' kids derive all the benefits of living in a close-knit
and caring community: special care when family members are ill, or
friendships with adults who model an honest faith. By contrast, when
congregations have too many divisive, manipulative, or hypocritical
members, the result may be confusion, mistrust, anger, or bitterness in
the PKs.

Over the long term, the crucial factor appears to be how conflicts
are handled by the parents. Do the parents help their children to
understand in ways that are appropriate to their level of awareness?
The world of a dissent-ridden congregation can be confusing, and
clergy children should not be left with only their imaginations as a
guide.

What do clergy parents teach about human nature, in what they
say and how they live? When pastors and their spouses live with
Christian integrity, hypocrisy can be viewed in its proper perspective.
Indeed, sometimes hypocrisy can even strengthen a PK's faith by
proving the parents' teaching about depending on an ever-faithful God
rather than reliance on inconsistent and fallible human beings. Again,
this assumes that clergy parents are demonstrating in their own lives
that there is, in fact, substance to Christianity.

The parishioners' influence on pastors' kids appears to be secondary to the quality of the foundation and ongoing support provided by the parents. This thought brings us full circle to the issue of how parents maintain family boundaries with respect to the congregation. Parents must make sure that the boundaries are not so poorly defined that their personal feelings intrude on the children's lives. Nor should the boundaries be so rigid that all discussion of problems in the church is thereby excluded. There is a happy medium that each family must strike with each child, depending on the child's curiosity and ability to understand.

The emphasis on the parents' role, however, does not eclipse the congregation entirely. To deny the influence of parishioners would be to make clergy parents wholly responsible for the way other people affect the lives of PKs. Clergy families do get hurt by the inappropriate behavior of church members, and the entire family must have the room to struggle with the pain. One clergy family who had been rejected by their congregation tried valiantly to deal with the situation constructively and in faith. But their efforts did not erase the PK's feelings:

■ My parents were hurt over it all, but they tried not to become bitter. They prayed a great deal both on their own and with us kids. They did share the circumstances with us older children and tried to help us understand, but it didn't stop me from getting bitter. It has taken years to get over the hurt.

This minister's child, weary of the cruel, hypocritical, and immature behavior he has seen in congregations, counsels them to find more constructive ways to express their dissatisfaction with the pastor:

■ I want the congregations of Christians in general to know how cruel they can be. Most of the time, if there are problems in the church, it's the minister's fault! This is not always true. The Bible says, "Before you take the speck out of your brother's eye, you should take the plank out of your own!" Most of the problems in the church are not the minister's fault. Too often, church members will act worse than kids. If they can't have their way, they will transfer to another church or make the minister and his family not very happy about these situations. My recommendation is for them to examine their own life before they criticize the minister, who is preaching the Word of God. If they still feel that they are in the right, they should talk to the minister instead of making his life miserable!

Clergy parents play a leading role in determining how church life influences their children, but a successful experience requires the full support of the rest of the cast. None of us can afford to neglect our part in the drama that is the life of a minister's child.

NOTES

1. See especially chapter 3, "A Family Within a Family." See also Edwin Friedman's earlier study *Generation to Generation: Family Process in Church and Synagogue* (New York: Guilford, 1985).

2. William Hulme, *Managing Stress in Ministry* (San Francisco: Harper & Row, 1985), 5.

3. Ibid.

4. Suzanne Geisler, *Jonathan Edwards to Aaron Burr, Jr.: From the Great Awakening to Democratic Politics* (New York: Edwin Mellen, 1981), 86–87.

EPILOGUE

The Reviews

CHAPTER TEN

A New Stage, a Better Script

So the drama goes. The stage is set, the script written, the players cast. Pastors' children play out their search for identity in the congregational setting, helped or hampered by numerous factors, only some of which have been discussed in this book. These include the appropriateness of social boundaries; the rules of communication; the prevalence of stereotypes and expectations; the children's individual characteristics; and relationships to parents, peers, and parishioners. No single factor takes precedence over the others. All work together, in different ways in different places, to frame the drama of an individual life.

Let's bring the curtain down at this point and ask for the reviews. Some pastors' children have truly loved growing up in a clergy home. They have not been victimized by stereotypes or congregational power plays. Their parents have been loving and consistent Christians who make the home a nurturing place. Here are a few of the "four-star" reviews received from PKs:

■ I really enjoy the privilege of being a PK and growing up in a Christian family.

■ I am grateful to God, who placed me in that role, for allowing me to grow up in an environment where Jesus Christ is not just a swear word.

■ I am glad I am a PK. It has given me a sound upbringing and a head start in life. It has shown me many things about life and people and how to cope. I am glad my father is who he is. He is a loving guy! He has shown me what I can be.

When everything works well, the PK may not even be conscious of being "different" from other kids:

> ■ I have always loved my family, my church, and life in general, so I don't think being a PK has been bad for me. Therefore it must have been positive. I never really thought before that "PK" meant anything much. I've just always been grateful to grow up in a godly family.

For some pastors' kids, the reviews are a little less rosy. They have seen the advantages and the disadvantages. Overall, they are happy to have been born PKs, but they have known firsthand the hardships that the role entails.

> ■ Although there have been bad times, I am glad that I am a PK.

> ■ For all the difficult times, there are great rewards also— spiritual inheritance and God-inspired parents are a blessing to any child!

> ■ Being a PK gives you experiences that no other teens will ever have. But basically, it's not a normal life at all.

> ■ It is definitely not an easy life, but I have enjoyed it, and it has great benefits (not forgetting the disadvantages). It's a hard life, but someone's got to do it—and why not me?

> ■ It is worth the trouble, heartache, and pain—I think.

Because they view their lives as "worth it" despite the difficulties, their counsel to pastors' families is to endure:

> ■ Just hold on!

> ■ Make the best of it.

> ■ We all go through stuff to learn and grow, and always for a reason. People have to hang in there and see things through and not be too quick to give up on things and people.

Such counsel may seem hollow to ministers' children who have been deeply hurt by parents or congregations. Their reviews are the most negative of all. Ask them, "If you could live your life over again, what would you do differently?" Their answer: They would find some way to avoid being born into a minister's family.

> ■ If I ever had a choice to be a PK, I'd definitely not be one. It is dreadful, pathetic, and a detriment to my Christian walk. Quite frankly, I hate it.

> ■ I would never do it again, if I had a choice, in regards to the hurts.

These pastors' kids also have counsel for prospective clergy:

- Don't do it.

- Don't join the ministry.

If you read entertainment reviews, you know how confusing they can be. One critic praises what another critic pans. It is virtually impossible to separate what is personal preference from what is "true" about a performance. In the end, the reviews themselves may offer little help for judging whether you would enjoy the play. So is there any more to be said?

Yes. Again, the point of taking an ecological approach is not to make a value judgment about whether it is good or bad to be born a pastor's child. We need to see the vast variety of elements that go into making up a person's experience and gain some sense of how these elements work together. With this knowledge we may be able to change things for the better.

To this end we need to look not only at PKs' "reviews," but also their recommendations. They have numerous suggestions and comments that can benefit congregations, clergy, and other PKs. I have grouped their recommendations generally according to the topics discussed in the previous chapters.

MAINTAINING CLEAR BOUNDARIES

In chapter 2 we looked at the importance of having clear social boundaries and gave several examples of boundary violations. Pastors' children are aware of the problems that come with having boundaries either too loosely or too rigidly defined.

At the most basic level, having appropriate boundaries means respecting the PK's individuality. This respect is central to all stages of identity development.

- As you raise your children, let them create their own individual identity.

- Allow each other to be comfortable with one's uniqueness.

In some cases individual identity is nearly obscured by stereotypes and unrealistic expectations. Pastors' kids want to be accepted for who they are as people, not for the role they play in the congregation:

- I think the fact that my parents loved me and cared about me as a person and not as a showpiece or exhibit or example for the church was vital in my youth.

- Don't put pressure on the kids to perform as PKs. Teach them to be themselves and help them to be able to. My parents really helped me to be myself, even to the point of sticking their necks out for me. This is very important!

Normal Treatment

In their own words, PKs want to be treated as "normal" kids, instead of being singled out as different in some way. "Normal" can mean many things. First, expectations should be realistic:

■ Give them unconditional love; don't put high unrealistic expectations on them; accept them as individuals. Teach the church to do the same.

■ They should treat their kids as "normal." In a way, I think it is important that we set an example because if we don't, this is reflected on my dad, and people may then not respect him. But I don't think unrealistic expectations should be placed on us.

■ Treat your kids as if they are *normal*—not too tough, not too lenient! We get enough "superkid" talk at church.

■ Don't expect your children to be perfect.

■ Don't have too high expectations of them.

Second, as individuals PKs will have their own opinions and point of view. They should be allowed to express these:

■ Let them be children and express themselves.

■ Give them room for expression.

■ Treat them like normal kids, and let them express themselves.

Third, we must remember that an important part of building identity is having some freedom to explore and to begin making decisions:

■ Don't let the church congregation rob your kids of dealing with adolescent issues. Let them be themselves even if that means doing some things you don't approve of. Kids, be yourselves.

■ I don't believe parents should smother their children and try to protect them so much from the world. I think the children should be able to freely taste the things of the world if they desire to. Parents should give advice on the right choices but not make the choices for their children.

■ Try not to be too critical. Find things they enjoy and let them go after them with passion.

■ I think that you shouldn't expect them to live a life the way you think they should. You can point them in the right direction, but they need to make the decision themselves.

■ Give them the freedom they need to make their own decisions. If they know that you trust them, this strengthens your relationship and builds self-confidence.

Christians First, PKs Second

The principle underlying all these suggestions is respect for the PK's boundaries as an individual. One extension of this principle is especially important to spiritual identity. The individual freedom the PKs suggest does not mean abandoning all standards of Christian conduct. This freedom is not absolute. But it does entail at least avoiding a *double standard:* If PKs are to be held to a standard, it should be one that applies to all Christians. In other words, PKs are to be treated as Christians first, rather than as PKs. When certain behaviors are expected or forbidden, it is because they are either appropriate or inappropriate for all Christians, not simply for PKs:

■ Don't tell them to act a certain way at church. Don't say, "Don't pull your sister's hair at church"; just say, "Don't pull your sister's hair."

■ One thing I don't like about being a PK is that people can believe you're being good because you're a PK, not because you're a Christian. But I generally was treated exactly the same as everyone else. Why shouldn't I be? I had nothing to do with Dad's being a pastor. To stereotype people because of their father or mother is stupid anyway. Moreover, I really enjoy church and youth group, not because I'm a PK, but because I'm a Christian.

■ Never put expectations on them as PKs, but as children of God in their own right.

■ My role is first to be a Christian and servant to Jesus Christ, not to be a servant to other people's expectations and attitudes toward me.

Avoiding a double standard yields wise counsel from one minister's child to others:

■ Be formed by God gradually, not by people instantly. God won't place expectations upon you that you can't handle; people will expect you to be something right away.

Another aspect of squeezing PKs into roles is viewing them as extensions of their parents' ministry. Pastors' kids should not be over-identified with their parents. They are individuals in their own right and should not be required, by virtue of being PKs, to be involved any more than other committed members of the church:

■ Don't use your children for "special" music or events more or less than others.

■ Parents should make a conscious effort to let their kids be as normal as possible. Don't force children to become "mini-pastors." All normal children will go through various stages of interest in church; let a PK go through these phases in a regular fashion. Don't expect too much. Pressure from parents to perform a certain way will most likely lead to rebellion.

■ Let them have activities apart from the church; don't force them to be in every single church event.

■ Clergy children are not extensions of their parents' ministry. They do not validate the quality of their careers or their faith. They are children, and they must be allowed the *space to fail* and ultimately succeed on their own.

Safe at Home

Safeguarding the PK's individuality entails other, closely related boundary issues. PKs recommend that clergy parents monitor how much the ministry is allowed to spill over into home life:

■ Try to make your home a haven of security—shut work out as much as possible. Children recognize more of the stress than you think they do!

■ Always be a family, and don't let circumstances and the church get between you. Tell your children what is going on, do your best, and love them, and they will love you in return.

■ Try to leave your work (ministry) at work. Ministers need to model Christian service, but there is a fine line between being a good example and bringing your work home constantly.

■ Try to keep the family low-key and out of the limelight. It makes life easier.

Clergy are urged to examine themselves to see whether they are still playing the role of the professional when they are at home:

■ Be a father to your kids when they need a father—not a pastor. Give fatherly advice, not a sermon.

Maintaining clear boundaries between church and home also means that clergy parents will not let pressures from the congregation determine how or when they discipline their children:

■ Don't punish any more or less than other parents.

■ Raise your children; don't let anyone else do it! This is to say, don't let a congregation dictate the discipline in your home. Set rules; follow them yourself—nothing is worse than a double standard. If you move, keep the rules the same; don't change them because the new church thinks you are too lenient or too strict. Don't conform to their rules: If it was okay before (such as movies or dancing), it's still okay now.

■ I feel it is wrong that the actions of the PKs are blamed on the parents. This only made me feel worse.

Everyone lives with expectations of some kind. Every person is influenced and shaped by relationships with other people. Keeping clear boundaries in the clergy family does not mean possessing a radical individualism. Such would entail rigid and inflexible boundaries, solid walls that would prevent ministers' children from being influenced in any way by parents or church members. This is as unrealistic as it is undesirable. But the opposite is no better: When no boundaries are defined at all, PKs are nearly "absorbed" by the will of others. Their identity becomes defined by how they fulfill their role expectations, rather than by whom God created them to be.

Somewhere there must be a realistic compromise between the two extremes. To have clear boundaries means to be influenced by others without being determined by them, to appreciate one's individuality without cutting oneself off from relationships. This is not unlike the balance inherent in the body of Christ, the church, in which no part is exclusive and the body cannnot function properly if one part eclipses the others.

KEEPING LINES OF COMMUNICATION OPEN

Good communication is essential if this balance is to be achieved and maintained. Again and again, pastors' children stress the need to talk, to receive their parents' emotional support. PKs know that their parents live under pressure; but as children, they also need to know that they can come to their parents for help and a listening ear.

■ Tell them how much you love them and make them feel important outside of the church.

■ Be a supportive family; communication is a vital part.

■ All I can say is always talk. Communication is one of the most important things. Even though it's hard, keep talking!

■ Be sure to keep the communication lines open. They're going to need your support and to know that they can talk to you about any problems they might be having. Communication with encouragement and love is the key.

■ They should let their children know that things can be talked out and solutions to problems can be worked out because clergy families are not perfect.

■ We do feel privileged to be children of men and women who have the call of God in their lives. But please explain things to your family when there is a need. Be there for them because PKs do have problems.

Good communication includes being open with children about problems in the church. In some churches there seems to be an unspoken rule that certain problems and feelings will not be discussed openly. But ministers' children pick up a great deal: from gossip, side comments made after the service, exchanged glances and facial expressions, and tense silences. They must feel free to talk with parents about whatever is going on because it is very likely to affect the PKs, directly or indirectly, in some way. Thus PKs request that their parents be open with them about difficult situations:

■ They should be open and honest with children and discuss difficulties.

■ Encourage openness and frank discussions. No topic of conversation should ever be off-limits.

■ Do explain church issues.

■ They should share difficult situations in the church.

■ Protect your family from the people, but don't keep them in the dark about what's going on. Kids need to know.

■ Don't hide things from your children. They will eventually hide things from you.

But being open does not mean "dumping" on the kids or venting anger on them or telling them every unpleasant detail. As we saw in chapter 9, parents should tailor their comments appropriately to a child's level of curiosity and knowledge.

■ First of all, communication is very important. You should be able to discuss things as a family. Second, I think you don't tell your kids everything. Some things shouldn't be discussed, and some things are for older children.

■ Don't fill their minds with adult concepts before they're ready regarding church difficulties.

■ If your children don't want to talk, don't pressure them.

It is a matter of satisfying the children's need to know as opposed to the parents' need to tell. This relies on the children's initiative to come and ask, and the parents' willingness to give a response that meets the children's needs.

Sometimes, however, parents should take the initiative and prepare children for what lies ahead. Clergy can anticipate stressful changes and family transitions. The parents should develop a strong tradition of good communication.

■ Include the children as appropriate in decisions to move, and educate them about their upcoming environment.

■ Be prepared for the strains of uprooting the family periodically by intentionally making the family unit strong through constant affirmation, attention, and sharing.

■ Try to explain and prepare young children for unexpected things that arise in the church that could ruin or postpone family plans, so that when it happens (and it will), they'll all at least have some understanding of it.

Maintaining clear boundaries and having good communication go hand in hand. If PKs feel that they have been trampled on, they must work this out in a supportive environment. Clergy parents who are able to keep the lines of communication open help their kids to sort through the many difficult identity issues that come with being a PK.

SETTING AND DEMONSTRATING FAMILY PRIORITIES

Perhaps the subject about which PKs have the most to recommend is family priorities. Many clergy parents seem unable to keep the boundaries between church and family clear. From their children's viewpoint, the message is that the family is not important enough to be valued and protected in its own right. Time and again, ministers' children advise clergy to put the family first:

■ Love your family or you've lost your ministry. Your family is the first fruit and proof of your ministry.

■ Family is first! The Bible repeatedly talks about raising children—if you have them, put them first!

■ Most important: Keep the family first! If need be, involve them in the ministry, but *never* put children in the back seat and ministry in the front.

■ Constantly emphasize that your children put their faith in God, not the church. The best way to show that is to serve God and not the church. This will help when you prioritize your life.

■ Keep your priorities right: (1) God, (2) spouse, (3) family, (4) job.

■ Get your priorities right! Your family needs you, and its demands (reasonable demands) should come first, before your ministry. They, too, are part of your church. You are *their* pastor too!

■ Children and marriage should come first. Priorities must be aligned and *followed*.

■ Make your family a priority and let your church know about it!

■ Don't forget your family. It is very easy to do. Don't become so involved in your church that you lose your kids without even knowing it. If you do, your kids will resent the church.

■ Get your priorities right: (1) God, (2) family, (3) church.

■ The children should come before the church.

■ Don't "win the world and lose your kids." They must be his highest priority after God and his wife, although the ministry will have to come first occasionally.

A verbal or mental commitment to making family life a top priority is not enough. Priorities must be demonstrated concretely if PKs are to feel important to their parents. This counsel comes in many forms:

■ Be aware of your children's needs, and give love.

■ Be sensitive to your children's feelings.

■ Make sure they get enough attention.

Ministers' kids need to know that their parents are thinking about them, considering their needs and feelings. How do they show this? One way is for a pastor to keep in touch with his children when he is traveling: "Always keep in touch when separated for any length of time; it keeps stability in the family." Billy Graham's biographer records that his children always knew that he was praying for them in his absence.[1] Dwight Moody's son Paul recalls this about his father:

> He remembered birthdays and wrote or telegraphed when away from home, no matter how busy he might be, and as might be imagined he delighted to give presents.[2]

It is delightful for children to realize that despite all the important things that occupy a minister's mind, they make it to the top of his list. Any way that clergy parents can demonstrate that they hold their kids in their thoughts will make them feel special.

Taking Time

Perhaps the most frequent suggestion, of course, is that clergy parents need to spend time with their children, both "quality" and "quantity" time:

■ Love your kids and spend plenty of time with them.

■ Spend quality time with them.

■ Take time out to be with your children. If they need you, don't ignore them.

■ The most important recommendation I can offer is to give your children quality time—making them feel valued.

■ Make sure they spend time with their children. This doesn't necessarily mean quality, but quantity time also.

The recommendation comes through at every age. The song "Cat's in the Cradle" that was popular some years ago tells the story of a man who was always too busy to spend time with his son. The song follows the pair through the different ages in the boy's life. Each time the son asks his dad to play with him, the father excuses himself and promises that they will play some other time. Finally, the son is old enough to leave home. The father is now obliged to ask the son to spend some time with him—but of course, the grown child is now too busy, just as his father had been. Is there any age in the life of pastors' children when it is not important for their parents to have time for them? PKs seem to suggest there is not:

■ Be with your children during their formative years.

■ Spend time with children when they are younger.

■ Spend extra time with their kids, even when they get older.

Spending time with the children does not mean always dragging the children into the parents' activities, but focusing on the children's interests: "Make sure you spend time with them doing things they want to do." This makes them feel important in their own right, especially when they must compete with the church for their parents' attention:

■ Most of all, take time for your children! Love them and let them know that they mean more than your congregation and that you'd choose them over the church any day!

■ Always have time for your children; don't neglect them for the needs of your church. Even at young ages, we are aware of being second best. Don't just say you love your children; give them the time and attention that show that you love them.

■ The parents should make sure that they set apart enough time to spend with their children. The kids need to know that the family comes first.

■ Try and spend as much time with your kids as you do with your congregation. Don't make your kids feel the congregation and their needs are more important.

Involved in Ministry

One way to spend time is to involve the kids in the ministry. Several PKs offer suggestions:

- Include them in your ministry without making a spectacle of them.

- Involve the kids, take them everywhere, do it together, constantly speak into their lives of their future with God, and above all make it the best family they could ever have.

- Make them a part of the ministry. Tell them they're important to the ministry.

- The ministry should be not just the mother and father; the children should be involved.

Because the children know the ministry is important in itself, as well as important to the parents personally, it can give them a feeling of specialness to be involved.

Recognizing Limitations

Taking time obviously means intentionally setting boundaries with the church. It begins with the clergy's recognizing their limitations:

- Take time for your family. Don't try to be everything to everyone in the church.

- I think you should remember to do family activities and not let the church run you. To clarify this, I think you should do as much as you can in your capabilities and *no more!*

Setting boundaries includes careful planning and organization and good follow-through:

- Ministers should have their church organized enough that not all the responsibilities are on them. Too many parents put their work above their kids, and being in the church doesn't make it easier. If the kids realize they are more important than the church and all its responsibilities, I believe the clergy family can survive and bring glory to God.

- It is very important that clergy families set aside time for the family—a time that is scheduled. The phone is taken off the hook, and the family is the most important.

Tasks that are to be done well usually take time. Parenting is no exception. Clergy parents cannot help their children develop a sense of worth if they do not spend time with them. Taking the time to listen and play are clear demonstrations that the family has an important place in the pastor's heart.

Spiritual Guidance

Another aspect of clergy family priorities is the spiritual guidance of the children. All Christian parents have this responsibility, but Christians also rely upon their pastors for spiritual direction. On whom do PKs rely to be their pastor? Clergy are expected to feed their flocks, yet they may neglect to include their own children. Pastors' kids ask that clergy parents tend to their spiritual needs and stress the importance of family devotions:

■ Do something about the children's spiritual lives as well as the members in the church.

■ Teach them how to have a heart for God. Don't just expect that they will grow into it.

■ Make sure they have a vital, dynamic, personal relationship with Jesus that is strong enough to cushion them from hurts and expectations.

■ Help your child develop a daily personal devotional walk with God.

■ He or she must spend enough time with his or her kids to ensure they are saved and walking with God. Special effort must be made to ensure that PKs have their own relationship with God, that they know him for themselves. Have regular family devotions.

Guidance does not mean coercion. PKs should be helped to develop a personal interest in matters of faith and not have these forced upon them. They cannot be bullied into heaven, but must give their devotion willingly.

■ They need to make sure that while they teach their children beliefs, the Bible, and Christian morals, they don't "shove it down their throats" and turn them away.

■ Spend much time with your children and let them explore the many facets of religion and life. Don't force them to make hasty decisions concerning religion; it will only draw them away from the church.

The foundation for this spiritual guidance is, of course, prayer. The entire clergy family can be brought together to pray regularly. But at the very least, it is the parents' responsibility to commit their children to God:

■ An active decision to meet and pray as a family is essential. All that can be shaken will be shaken, so be aware and act immediately when problems arise. Love them and pray for them. Bring them up in the way of the Lord, and when they are older, they will not depart from it!

■ My parents checked regularly on my spiritual growth and quickly got down on their knees if they saw any rough patches.

■ I recommend that before you even enter the ministry, you pray for your spouse and your children (born or not).

■ Just lay your children on the altar daily.

We see that there are many ways for clergy parents to show that their children are important: being mindful of their needs and feelings, spending time with them, being committed to their spiritual well-being. These are vital links in the chain of interactions that help PKs establish secure identities as individuals and as Christians.

A TRUE EXAMPLE OF CHRISTIAN CHARACTER

As we saw in chapter 9, hypocrisy in the minister's home can seriously damage a PK's spiritual identity. How can parents provide solid spiritual guidance when their lives are marred by flagrant inconsistency? Ministers' children emphasize how crucial it is that clergy parents model authentic faith in their own lives. To one PK, this factor is far more important than the amount of time the family spends together:

■ There is much emphasis on PKs failing because of lack of time with them—I don't believe this. It's more important for parents to be valid people and have a real relationship with God and to know your kids at the crucial times, such as puberty, and to have a good marriage. PKs need a challenge and to be taught a committed, self-sacrificing lifestyle. Give them love, and they'll turn into productive people. The killer is hypocrisy.

Parents who act hypocritically give their children no foundation for believing that there is substance to faith. But clergy who practice what they preach are trustworthy role models for their children.

Ministry cannot be just a role. Religion cannot be moral play-acting. It must be a way of life, the natural expression of the parents' identity. Pastors' kids want parents to be both "real" people and people of real Christian character:

■ Be real with your kids and just love them!

■ Be as real as you possibly can. God called you to be you long before He called you to ministry! And let everyone in your family be real, too.

■ Don't be unreal or have a plastic existence.

■ Teach and demonstrate high morals, values, and standards. Show your children how important the Bible is to you and to the family as a whole. Don't compromise standards just to give in to the situation. Children look back and remember the character of their parents.

■ "Love the Lord your God with all your heart, mind, soul, and strength. Love your neighbor as yourself." This is Christianity.

When clergy parents do not live out a consistent faith, their children may be left with gaps in their spiritual development:

■ Devotions in our home while growing up were at best a pain! At no other time did Christianity seem relevant in our home. Neither of my parents ever spoke with me about my personal relationship with God. But what's so interesting is that this is the most difficult area of my life today! To a great degree, I have failed at the very same point my parents did.

A highly visible demonstration of Christian character is the strength of the parents' marriage:

■ I believe the most important thing for a clergy family is a strong, loving marriage that is able to deal with the real issues of life in a positive way. They need to live out what they believe, facing their own weaknesses honestly with a strong emphasis on having fun together.

Pastors' kids want their parents' guidance in the faith. But this guidance must be confirmed by a living demonstration of what is taught. Without this, the teaching is hollow, and PKs will very likely struggle with their commitment.

RECEIVING SUPPORT FROM OTHERS

Some weaknesses in a PK's development resulting from parental faults can be strengthened through church members who are able to provide the kind of support and guidance they need. Pastors' children who have been fortunate enough to have involved, caring parents and supportive adults in the congregation are truly grateful for having been born into ministry. Where the feeling of parental support is missing, others may provide some consolation. This PK is thankful for the patient listening ear of his youth pastor:

■ I think God makes up the void that is left by parents who are busy with church involvement. I feel that God has abundantly made up for what I felt I had missed. Now that I am older, I have been able to put that into perspective and appreciate its value. I had great support from our youth pastor, who stopped to listen. That's what I needed. This helped greatly, and I am convinced this is what helped me to turn away from my rebellious phase and turn back to God.

If being ministers' kids means being different, it makes sense that they would find support in getting together with other PKs:

■ It's great being with kids who have been through the same things.

■ Support groups are a must. We shouldn't have to cope on our own. I greatly appreciate PK camp and without it would not be the same person I am today, living for God and happy in his will.

■ PK camps are great!

Besides examining their own roles in the lives of PKs, clergy and congregations can encourage the development of support systems for them. Special camps for PKs have been remarkably successful in providing a sense of belonging—and even sanity. Others in the community may be willing to sponsor support groups. Whatever measures are taken, they will be a tangible affirmation of the special needs of ministers' kids.

THE ROAD TO WHOLENESS

The very purpose of this book has been to affirm those special needs. Congregations and prospective clergy must realize that the environment of ministry is a special context that can either enhance or complicate a child's emotional development. Each chapter in this book has been devoted to showing a distinctive aspect of the "ecology" that constitutes the PK's world. If the painful aspects have appeared to receive greater emphasis, it is because those who have been violated in some way as pastors' kids are most in need of empathy and hope. Hope comes, first, in their recognizing that others have shared similar experiences. Some PKs in my survey needed to know that their experiences were not unique—that they were not crazy people, that God did not somehow single them out from the rest of humanity to suffer a peculiar fate.

Beyond this, however, hope comes from knowing that some of those who have been hurt have found a road to wholeness. Healing begins with an honest recognition of the problem as well as one's feelings about it. This PK has discovered his deeply rooted anger toward the church—and though he does not yet express it openly, he is at least giving himself permission to feel it:

■ In essence I am still in the "good PK trap." Right now my heart hates the church and finds little value in the study of Scripture or the church's teachings. Yet I feel trapped in the church. If I were to disown the church openly, I would fear reflection on my family of origin. I also fear what my children would feel. As I look back, I say, "What a sad, co-dependent, dysfunctional relationship I have developed with the church and my family." I don't think this is only the result of being a PK, but in my case being a pastor's kid probably made it worse. I am angry, which is therapeutic in that I can finally see the problem. I guess I am just beginning my journey.

Others have come a little farther in the journey. They have learned, often through therapy, the ability to speak the truth about their feelings. This PK, having expressed her anger, has begun the process of forgiveness. Although she has not reached her ultimate goal, her gradual emotional healing is itself a message of hope:

■ Where am I now? Well, I have fought fiercely to love God in spite of my anger and cynicism surrounding organized Christianity. My tools for fighting have been my therapy, a sense of God's presence, a growing consciousness of the good parts of what it meant to grow up as a minister's daughter, a gradual releasing of anger at pettiness through expressing, being heard, and affirmed, and gradually letting go. After a period of feeling hurt and angry, I find I am gradually forgiving my parents for being human while in a position of sainthood, forgiving others for wanting too much of them and of me, forgiving myself for my own shortcomings. I forgive them, not because I think I should, but because there is far too much in life that I love to allow myself to feel only the hurts of the past and the inadequacies I felt because of them.

I still feel a need to protect my parents from my thoughts, a fact that is expressed most eloquently by a thought that just slipped through my mind: "I hope my parents never get ahold of this letter." Letting them see honestly what I see may be my final hurdle—or perhaps my ongoing task.

Nothing in this book should be taken as the final word on the subject. These are the observations and interpretations of many ministers' children, brought together in one place, as filtered through one writer's mind. As such, the ideas presented here are intended to be a catalyst for reflection and change.

To borrow a phrase, a truly great play is never written, but rewritten. We brought the curtain down to hear the reviews, but it is time to raise it again. The next act begins. How will it go? Will we continue with the same kind of stage direction, mouthing the same script? It is my prayer that, where needed, this book will help clergy and congregations to rewrite their roles in the lives of ministers' children and rebuild the settings in which the dramas are played out. But most of all, I hope that with God's grace, pastors' kids who have lived out tragic scripts will be encouraged to bring the next act of the drama to a healing resolution.

NOTES

1. John Pollock, *Billy Graham: Evangelist to the World* (San Francisco: Harper & Row, 1979), 143.
2. Paul D. Moody, *My Father: An Intimate Portrait of Dwight Moody* (Boston: Little, Brown, 1938), 78.

Index